The Great
MANGO
Book

THE GREAT MANGO BOOK

Allen Susser

Photography by
Greg Schneider

TEN SPEED PRESS
Berkeley / Toronto

Dedicated to my wife, Judi,
and my girls, Deanna and Liza

Ten Speed Press
P.O. Box 7123
Berkeley, California 94707
www.tenspeed.com

Distributed in Australia by Simon and Schuster Australia,
in Canada by Ten Speed Press Canada, in New Zealand by
Southern Publishers Group, in South Africa by Real
Books, in Southeast Asia by Berkeley Books, and in the
United Kingdom and Europe by Airlift Book Company.

Cover design by Stefanie Hermsdorf
Book design by Nancy Austin
Food and Prop Styling by Allen Susser
"Varieties of Mangos" text with Richard Campbell

Library of Congress Cataloging-in-Publication Data
  Susser, Allen.
    The great mango book / Allen Susser; photography
by Greg Schneider.
      p. cm.
  Includes bibliographical references and index.
    ISBN 1-58008-204-1
    1. Cookery (Mangos) 2. Mango. I. Title.
  TX813.M35 S87 2001
  641.6'444—dc21   2001003543

First printing, 2001

Printed in Hong Kong

1 2 3 4 5 6 7 8 9 10 — 06 05 04 03 02 01

Contents

Preface - vi

Introduction - viii

VARIETIES OF MANGOS - 1

COOKING WITH MANGOS - 61

Beverages & Starters - 69

Main Dishes - 87

Condiments - 103

Desserts - 119

Bibliography - 136

Index - 137

Preface

My mango affair started back in college. The South Miami neighborhood I lived in was filled with mango trees. As many of the folks from the Islands did, on a hot summer day I would relax under the shade of a mango tree, pluck and taste its fruit. It was pure summer. In the evenings, I often went to a Cuban juice bar in Coconut Grove. My favorite was the frozen mango batido (a mango milkshake): fresh sliced mango, ice, and milk, with a touch of honey, all whirled together in a blender. Those batidos were a sweet, lush, cooling pleasure. Little did I realize then how important mangos would become to me.

When I opened my restaurant, Chef Allen's, naturally I used locally-grown mangos on the menu. One of my favorite dishes was grilled wahoo (a local white-fleshed game fish) with fricassee of lobster, mango, and coconut rum. I also made a mango tart, a takeoff on a classic French tart.

Then, several years ago at a mango festival in Miami, I met Dr. Richard Campbell, the curator of tropical fruits for Fairchild Tropical Gardens. He was directing a sampling for the attendants of a Mango Morning event. About 150 different varieties of mangos were on display. I was there among other mango enthusiasts, who had volunteered to cook some of their favorite recipes. In exchange for one of my mango cream-filled doughnuts, Dr. Campbell brought me one of his prized Indian Alphonse mangos to taste—my first sampling of an Indian mango. It was a small, yellow-skinned fruit with a deep, sunset-yellow flesh. This was a mango to be reckoned with, a chef's mango, with deep, flavorful notes of spice, and hints of apricot, musk, pumpkin, and vanilla. I wanted more. What about the other mangos and their flavors? I tasted ten more varieties. I was hooked. This new palette of flavors exhilarated me.

Needless to say, Richard and I soon became great friends. And what a beautiful beginning it was: I'd often drop by Fairchild Gardens where, as we toured the orchards, Richard would teach me about the botanical and horticultural life of the mango. Clever man that he is, Richard made sure I never left empty-handed. Armed with a basket brimming with yellow, green, or crimson mangos, I'd rush home and into the kitchen to prepare a feast with my delicious loot. Like any true friendship, ours was two-way: while Chicken and Green Mango Stew simmered on the stove or the aroma of warm Country Mango Tarts filled my home, I'd pick up the phone and invite Richard to come on over.

One night, after enjoying a meal made with three mangos as diverse in appearance, aromas, textures and flavors as their countries of origin, I became determined to introduce others to the diversity of this beautiful fruit. I started with my family and friends; then moved onto diners at my restaurant, Chef Allen's; and now onto you. I hope that not only will this book familiarize you with the different varieties of mangos available in your local gourmet shops and grocery stores, but that the mangos you'll find there, will bring you as much joy as they have me—whether cooked up in batch of Mango-Peach Marmalade, wrapped in a thin slice of prosciutto, or eaten right out of your hand.

A basketful of thanks to Richard Campbell for sharing his excitement of this simple fruit—the mango. To my staff at Chef Allen's: Theo, Doreen, Craig, Tom, Joe, Stephan, Ian, and Susan for their help in getting through my years of mango madness. To the Mango Gang. To my friends Laleau, Tomas, Dawn, Gabriel, Yada, Richard, and Trupti who related their personal passions of growing up with mangos in hometowns around the world—from Latin America to the Caribbean to India. To Greg for bringing the mangos to life through his lens. To Meghan, my editor, whose pen kept me focused. To Dennis at Ten Speed for being himself. Finally to Phil, whose never ending quest for adventure and the exotic enabled me to bring this book to you, the reader.

Allen Susser and Richard Campbell at the Fairchild Tropical Gardens in Miami, Florida

Introduction

The word is out that I'll trade mangos for dinner. It's a simple deal: dinner for two at Chef Allen's for a wheelbarrow of mangos. That might seem like a steep bounty for this humble fruit, but not in South Florida. It's a challenge Miamians happily rise to every summer, when mangos are plentiful in backyards and groves alike. The pride of owning a mango tree turns to a passion as the trees begin to ripen late in June.

Only the immediate family members are allowed to eat the first few fruits from their tree. During the following couple of weeks, mangos are handed out to close friends and relatives. Then, as the tree fills with sweet, ripe mangos, small bags of the fruit are given to even the most casual acquaintances. Home cooks are happy, trading mango jam recipes and tips for baking mango pies. Just when they feel they have the ripening fruit tree under control, suddenly it's filled with anywhere from seventy-five to two hundred lush, crimson mangos. That's when it's time to call the chef! "I've got four shopping bags filed with mangos," the caller says, "Is that enough for dinner?" Our answer: "Come on in and we will take them off your hands."

Then, they start arriving at my back door. I love it. Pastel and greenish-yellow-skinned Keitt mangos, with their firm and juicy skin, have a slight berry aroma. Nam Doc Mai mangos, with their canary yellow skin and tender flesh, have a citrusy, tropical-fruit flavor. And the ubiquitous Tommy Atkinses, with their red-blushed skin, have a juicy, deep yellow flesh, with rich flavors and floral aromas.

What do we do with all this lush fruit? It's mango madness. Our menu is filled with mangos all summer long: Mango-Shrimp Cocktail, Mango and Tuna Sashimi Salad, Grilled Mahimahi with Mango Sauce, Panfried Soft-Shell Crabs with Green Mango Slaw, Mango Lassi, Green Mango Pickle, Mango Chutney, and on through to Mango Split with Rum-Caramel Sauce and Macadamia Nuts.

Each mango offers a different flavor, texture, and color and dictates its own culinary direction. The Kyo Savoy variety, for example, is better when eaten green. In its native land of Thailand, this mango is usually matched with hot, salty, sour, and sweet flavors and spices. There, street vendors sell green mangos with a choice of pungent toppings. The Sandersha, an Indian variety, is cooked when still green in chutneys that include exotic spices such as cardamom, asafoetida, and fenugreek. Other mangos, including many of the Florida varieties, are best eaten ripe and sweet in recipes such as Crab and Mango Salad and Mango Cobbler.

The King of Fruits

With such great variety in flavor and appearance, it's no surprise that the growing range of mangos extends from the groves of South Florida through the Caribbean, and from South America to Southeast Asia. Truly the king of fruits, the mango has melted into the cuisines, cultures, and hearts of people around the world.

The species name of the mango is *Mangiferi indica*, which means "an Indian plant bearing mangos." It is thought to have originated over five thousand years ago in the Hindo-Berma region, though wild varieties are known to be indigenous to the Malay Archipelago. The word *mango* is a corruption of the Portugese *manga*. The first mention of the word *mango* appeared in English in 1582.

The mango is the most auspicious and yet utilitarian tree in India, where the history of its cultivation goes back at least four thousand years. Its popularity can be felt in every facet of Indian life and culture. People, places, and even musical notes are named after this fruit. The mango also appears as a symbol and attribute of many gods and goddesses in Hinduism, Buddhism, and Jainism.

For a plant with such a long history of cultivation, the mango's spread outside its native countries was surprisingly slow. It was not introduced into East Asia until the Buddhist period, in the fourth or fifth century B.C. Chinese history traces the mango to that same period, around 645 B.C. Alexander the Great found mangos in the Indus Valley in 327 B.C. Mangos were brought to the Philippines by Islamic missionaries sometime between 1400 and 1450.

Cultivation of the mango began slowly moving westward when the people of India started to trade spices, mangos and other tropical fruits with Westerners. The Portuguese, who landed in Calcutta in 1498, were the first to establish a mango trade. They are also credited with bringing the mango to Brazil during the sixteenth century. By 1742, mangos had been introduced to port cities from Barbados to Rio de Janeiro.

In 1782, a British captain of the HMS *Flora* captured, off Jamaica, a French ship that was sailing to Haiti. The French ship was carrying spice plants and seeds, including mangos. The mango seeds were planted near Garden Town in the parish of St. Andrews, Jamaica, and the resulting seedlings were numbered. The only surviving plant was "number 11"—thus the Number 11 mango which eventually became ubiquitous in the Islands. In 1869, other grafted varieties were imported from India and, in all, twenty-two varieties were introduced in Jamaica.

Mexico owes its mango production to two sources. First, mangos were brought by Spanish galleons trading between Manila and Acapulco in the early seventeenth century. Then, in the early nineteenth century, other varieties came from the West Indies. In the early 1800s, the Mexican mango was introduced into Hawaii though other varieties such as the Pirie from India, the Carabao from the Philippines, and the Julie from Jamaica, have come to Hawaii more recently.

The first attempt to introduce the mango into the United States came in 1833, when pioneer Henry Perrine

brought plants to Florida; unfortunately, following his death in 1840, these plants failed due to neglect. Reintroduction did not follow until 1861, when the Number 11 mango was brought in from Cuba and planted near the Miami river. In 1889, the U.S. Department of Agriculture imported the first grafted mangos from Bombay, India and sent them on to homesteaders in South Florida. Of these mangos, the only to survive the freeze of 1894–95 was the Mulgoba which originally fruited in 1898. The Mulgoba is famous as the first true mango variety to have fruited in Florida and was the mother of the Haden, now one of the most popular mangos not just in South Florida, but throughout the Americas.

The mango has had a tumultuous history in Florida, particularly in Miami. In 1900, Henry Flagler, a railroad baron and partner of the Rockefellers, provided land for the Miami Plant Introduction Garden. David Fairchild, who later founded the USDA Office of Foreign Seed and Plant Introduction, was brought on to oversee the garden and soon planted specimens from the U.S. Department of Agriculture's shipment. The great hurricane of 1926 wiped out much of the garden, along with much of Miami. Luckily, the mango had become well-established throughout the South Florida area, and thus survived the shock. History repeated itself in 1992, when much of South Florida and its mango crop were devastated by Hurricane Andrew. Today, Miami and the mango are more vibrant than ever. Miami's culturally diverse population includes people of Caribbean, Latin, South American, Indian, and Southeast Asian descent—all enormous fans of this exquisite fruit— making the city a hotbed of mango excitement.

Today, over 150 varieties of mango are grown in the backyards and groves of Florida. In South Florida each summer, a host of mango events range from Mango Month at Fairchild Tropical Gardens to the Tropical Ag Fiesta. And around the world, festivals in India, Brazil, Malaysia, and South Africa attract mango enthusiasts with tastings, horticultural seminars, and cooking classes. The world loves mangos.

Botany and Cultivation

The mango is a member of the cashew family (*Anacardiaceae*) of flowering plants; other species within the same family include the pistachio tree, the Peruvian pepper tree, and poison ivy.

An evergreen, the height and shape of the mango tree varies considerably among the different varieties. The leaves are thick, leathery, and oblong in shape, with short, pointed ends. Though purple when young, the leaves usually mature to a deep green. The small, pinkish-white flowers appear from December to March, depending on weather conditions, and are borne in large panicles (loosely branched flower clusters forming a pyramid-like shape) on or near the end of branchlets. Each panicle holds fifteen hundred or more flowers. If the fruit does not set, a second or even third bloom might occur before it does eventually set.

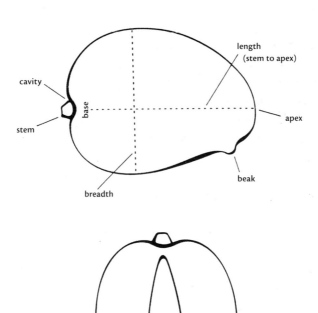

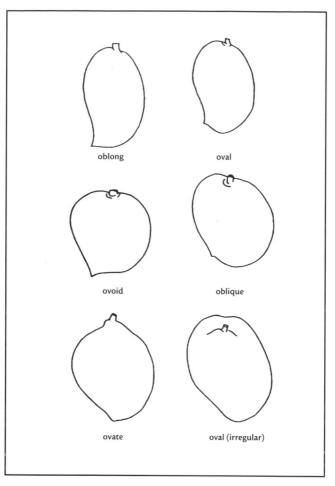

oblong

oval

ovoid

oblique

ovate

oval (irregular)

Botanically, the fruit is a drupe, consisting of an outer skin, a fleshy edible portion, and a stone enclosing a single seed.

Mangos can range from 2 to 10 inches in length and from 4 ounces to 5 pounds in weight; their shape can vary from flat, to round, to long and slender.

The color of a mango's skin depends on its variety. Saigon types are generally more yellowish green than the bright red-cheeked Indian varieties with their brilliant yellow backgrounds. Fruits hanging in the sunlight are usually brighter in color than those inside the canopy of the same tree. The fruit's color might be mottled, with spots or blotches of reds, yellows, or greens and its surface may be waxy or sprinkled with large, dark pores, or "corky dots" as they are often referred to.

The aroma of the fruit is pleasant and alluring; the flesh ranges from yellow to deep orange. The best varieties are almost fiberless, melting in texture, and have rich, luscious, semi-spicy flavors.

Mangos can be raised from seed or propagated by grating: the joining of a woody shoot from a mature tree with a seedling. This process creates an exact copy of the mother tree. (A mango plant grown from a seed will rarely be the same variety as its mother plant.) When a new seedling (hybrid) is recognized, described, named, and propagated by grafting, it's referred to as having been "selected" from its parent varieties. Mango "cultivars," are these recognized and named selections.

Once a tree is developed, mangos are produced singly or in clusters. In the Northern Hemisphere they mature from late May to September. The mango tree thrives in tropical and subtropical climates, particularly in places with good rainfall followed by a dry season to stimulate fruit production. Extreme conditions often have adverse effects on the mango; it cannot withstand severe frost or high temperatures with low humidity and high wind.

Comfort Food

I've never seen so many cultures so passionate about a fruit. For millions of people throughout the world, the mango is a comfort food, one of those comestibles that nourish both body and soul.

In Bangkok, Thailand, mangos are sold both ripe and green by street vendors. At many stands, ripe mangos are piled high in neat triangular stacks, their stems still covered with sap. Nearby are large aluminum bowls filled with translucent sticky rice, ready to be served with the just-peeled flesh. Mature green mangos, crunchy and very tart, are usually cut into chunks or julienned with a hand raspier (a small, sharp cutting tool). The shredded flesh is served with a variety of sauces, ranging from salty to sweet, but always with a little heat. In Thailand, marketplace vendors also add the tightly-closed mango blossoms to spicy soups.

On the streets of Manila in the Philippines, vendors sell small, convenient hand pouches filled with the aromatic Carabao mango and a sauce of fermented shrimp, garlic, and turmeric. This green mango, almost blue in skin color, is quickly hand peeled. The fruit is sliced vertically with a sharp blade inserted to the stone. The flesh is sliced away from the stone, leaving just a little mango attached at the bottom. Locals eat the mango by pulling off a slice and dipping it into the sauce.

In Vietnam, crisp green, salted mango slices are sold spiked with green chilies. And in the Pacific coastal regions of Mexico, the slightly acidic green Oro mango is cut up and seasoned with salt and red pequin chile powder. In Tabasco, families consume mangos *en plancha*: peeled, lightly salted, and impaled on a round, wooden stick. The mango is cut to look somewhat like a pineapple, with wedges of fruit cut away from the stone from the top down to the base.

In Brazil, you can't miss the stylish juice bars serving spicy Rosa mango juice, usually mixed with orange juice. In Florida, open-air juice bars and Latin cafeterias serve lush, ripe Hadens and Tommy Atkinses in mango shakes called batidos. Another summer treat are the baskets of scented mangos from backyard trees that friends and well-wishers send each other as a gesture of friendship and good will. In South Florida, mangos are not only street food but part of the language. The Latin community shows its passion for the fruit with several common slang phrases: *Arroz con mango* (total confusion), *¡Le zumba el mango!* ("That takes the cake"), *¡Me mango!* ("take me for a fool!"), and *Eso es conger mango bajito* ("like taking candy from a baby").

The Caribbean has many roadside stands where fruit juices are poured over cones of crushed ice—mango is one of the most popular flavors. Throughout Jamaica the red-and-yellow-skinned, fibrous but juicy Number 11 mangos are smashed gently on the ground, then rolled in the palm of the hand until all the pulp is evenly distributed. The stem is then cut or bitten off, and the sweet juice of the mango is sucked out.

In India, the mango is not only regarded as a delicious fruit, but as an object of celebration. The tribal people of northeastern India celebrate the first blush of the mango blossoms as well as the first mangos of the season. Before this "first-fruit ceremony," it is strictly forbidden to eat mangos. During the mango season throughout India, large picnics are organized in mango orchards, where mangos are picked, cooled in buckets of ice water, and eaten out of hand. The mango motif is used as a symbol of desire and plenty in textiles, paintings, and jewelry. In fact, in his *Kama Sutra*, Sage Vatsyayana advises lovers to drink the refreshing juices of mango and other fruits before sexual play. Indians also use mango idioms to express themselves: "A ripe mango at the point of dropping" refers to an old person at the point of death. "The mango is sourer near the stone" means that the real state of something can only be known if you go deeply into it.

The marketplaces in India are filled with dealers who display a vast array of mango varieties, including ripe mangos desserts, green mangos for chutneys, and green mangos for eating out of hand. An amazing range of mango products are offered, ranging from mango pickles and amchoor (green mango powder), to jarred chutneys. Bottled mango juices and drinks called squash are also popular.

Most of the preferred varieties in India have yellow skin; Europeans prefer yellow-skinned mangos with a red blush, and Americans like red-skinned fruit. But all around the world, mangos are enjoyed as a voluptuous and satisfying food.

VARIETIES

OF

MANGO

Ah Ping

Ah Ping originated as a seedling in a home garden in
Molokai, Hawaii. This attractive fruit has a bright red to
crimson blush on a yellow to green background. The color
can be quite similar to the Haden. These oblong mangos
range in size from 1 to 2 pounds and ripen at the beginning
of the mango season. They are eaten when fully ripe and
aromatic, when the dark orange flesh is sweet and rich with
flavor. Ah Ping has never attained a presence outside of
Hawaii, but within the islands it is highly appreciated and
recommended for planting in home gardens.

**Tasting Notes: A lush, slightly grassy tropical scent with a
pronounced peach flavor and a hint of roses.**

Alampur Baneshan

Alampur Baneshan originated in the Andhra Pradesh
region of North India, and is considered one of the finest
dessert mangos in India. The fruit are large, oblique and
oblong, averaging from 14 to 16 ounces. The skin is green,
even when fully mature, and is overlaid with characteristic
corky dots covering the fruit surface. As with most of the
other fine dessert mangos of India, Alampur Baneshan is
best harvested when hard and green, then ripened at
room temperature. Thus, this mango develops an exceptionally strong flavor with many levels, from deep and
resinous to intensely sweet. This is a mango for the connois-
seur, not the beginner. The fruit are uncommon outside
India, and due to their color, limited yield, and tendency to
split open before picking, it is unlikely that they will enter
the international export market.

**Tasting Notes: Pungent, aromatic notes of clove and
cinnamon, and a custard-smooth flesh flavored with
honey, red pepper, and allspice.**

Alphonse

Alphonse (often called Alphonso) is one of the best Indian dessert mangos. Originating in Goa, Alphonse usually weighs around 10 ounces, with an ovate-oblique shape. The fruit can be green or bright yellow, depending on the environmental conditions, and often has a pink blush on the sun-exposed shoulder. The ripening fruit are wonderfully perfumed, and the flavor is intensely sweet, rich, and full, with multiple aromatic overtones. Alphonse is called "sweet-sweet" by locals, and there is no fiber in the melting orange flesh. Alphonse is thought to be best suited for fresh consumption, and is exported from India to specialty markets in Europe. It is harvested at the mature green stage and should not be refrigerated prior to ripening. Instead, the fruit should be stored at 70°F for the optimal development of flavor and aroma.

Tasting Notes: Intense aromatic characteristics of apricot, mint, and papaya, with a flavorful, creamy flesh tasting of vanilla and spice.

Anderson

Anderson was selected in Miami the 1940s. The shape of the Anderson is unique: long, slender, and sigmoid. Unusually large, the fruits weigh from 46 to 60 ounces each. The stem is elongated, adding to its characteristic shape. The skin is typically greenish-yellow, with a crimson or dark red blush when exposed to the sun. The skin is thick and tough, the flesh soft, juicy, and pale yellow. The parents of Anderson are not known, but it has many of the characteristics of an Indian pickling mango. The fruit is best used for chutney or achar. Due to its large size and long shape, this mango has a tendency to split on the tree.

Tasting Notes: A surprisingly light citrus aroma, with layered flavors of pineapple, peach, and candied lime rind.

Ataulfo

Ataulfo burst onto the mango scene in recent years as an import from Mexico. Selected in the Yucatán region, it has been a favorite there for decades. It has many of the characteristics of Indochinese mangos, and probably owes its heritage to that region. The fruit are slender and sigmoid, weighing between 6 and 8 ounces. They are canary yellow, with a deep yellow flesh that has slight acidity to complement its spicy and sweet flavor. There is no fiber in the flesh, yet the flesh is firm and resistant to handling. Due to its distinctive flavor, Ataulfo has earned a prominent place among the group of export mangos from Mexico. This mango is helping to build an increasing market for high-quality yellow mangos in the United States and beyond.

Tasting Notes: A bright red grape aroma, with a slight tangerine taste and a pleasant peach finish.

Baptiste

Baptiste was selected in Haiti, where it is grown on commercial scale for the local market. It is mostly unknown beyond the island. The fruit are oval, with a smooth, non-waxy skin, and weigh from 8 to 16 ounces. They are bright yellow to orange and have no blush. The flesh is extremely firm, with surprisingly little fiber. The flesh is a deep orange, with a mild and sweet flavor. In Haiti, the trees are often grown from seed. There have been some limited exports of Baptiste to the United States, but due to inconsistent supply and quality and the unfamiliarity of the consumer with this fruit, exports have not been successful. The firm flesh holds its shape on cutting and heating, which makes this variety well-suited for fruit salads and cooking.

Tasting Notes: A pleasant lime and pine aroma, with a slightly sweet watermelon flavor and a mild cinnamon-heat aftertaste.

Bombay

Bombay is a traditional selection from Jamaica. As the name suggests, it probably originated from seeds brought to the island by early Indian immigrants. The fruit are similar in shape, taste, and habit to the Paheri of India and the Pirie, or Pairi, found in the Caribbean. The fruit range from 10 to 12 ounces and are a deep green color when fully ripe. When exposed to the sun, they often develop a red shoulder. The skin is smooth, and the flesh deep orange, melting, and juicy with little fiber. The flavor is rich and spicy, reminiscent of the finest of Indian dessert mangos. Due to a susceptibility to disease, the trees typically bear only a few fruit each year but fetch good prices in Caribbean markets. Bombay is rarely found in the specialty markets of North America and Europe. The fruit may be deeply scored around the middle and can be twisted to separate. The sweet, delectable flesh of the two halves can then be spooned out, leaving only the pit and the skin.

Tasting Notes: A deep floral aroma, with a lovely balance of spiced fruits, pears, and ripe peaches.

Cambodiana

Cambodiana was among the earliest of the Indochinese mango seedlings sent to Miami from the Philippines by David Fairchild in 1902. The fruit are oblong to ovate, with an undulating and lightly waxed skin. Small in size, they range from 8 to 12 ounces. When ripe, the fruit are canary yellow with no blush. The lemon-yellow flesh is completely without fiber, soft, and melting with an aromatic, rich, and slightly tangy flavor. The taste is excellent, making it useful in culinary applications where a distinctive flavor is desired. Due to their small size and poor storage characteristics, Cambodiana are not good candidates for export to the United States and Europe. But Cambodiana and similar mangos are sold in local markets around the world, where they are prized for their flavor and versatility.

Tasting Notes: A sweet aroma of dried fruit and anise, with a mild peachy flavor and a big banana finish.

Carabao

Carabao, the most prevalent mango cultivar in the Philippines, can be found in markets throughout Southeast Asia. It is usually eaten ripe as a dessert mango, but it is also used when mature and green. The fruit are long and slender, with a bluntly pointed apex, and are usually rather small, 10 to 14 ounces. Light green when unripe, they gradually change to a lemon or canary yellow when ripe. The flesh is completely without fiber, soft, and juicy, with a sweet and aromatic flavor and a slight tartness. Carabao is exported to Asia and Europe, but is not common, and is usually available only in ethnic markets. The fruit are often sliced and preserved in a sugar syrup. Two Mexican mangos, Manila and Ataulfo, are often compared to Carabao in terms of size, color, and flavor. Although there are some distinctions, these cultivars are similar enough to be used in much the same ways.

Tasting Notes: Plush citrus, fruit, and ginger flavors, with lingering hints of lemon and pineapple.

Cushman

Due to Cushman's unique and distinctive appearance, it is often mistaken for a grapefruit. It was selected in Miami in the 1930s and has been grown on a semi-commercial basis by small farmers in Florida for many years. The fruit are rounded and large, weighing from 25 to 35 ounces. The skin is completely yellow, with no blush, and characteristic corky dots on the surface. The flesh is deep yellow, firm, and juicy, with no fiber. Its flavor is excellent, sweet and rich, making it one of the best of the end-of-the-middle-season mangos. Cushman is only marketed in South Florida in midsummer.

Tasting Notes: A concentrated sweet fruit and spice nose, with tropical flavors of guava, banana, and toasted almond.

Dasheri

Dasheri is a traditional dessert cultivar from North India. The fruit are oblong in shape and rather small in size, usually weighing from 8 to 10 ounces. The fruit are canary yellow when ripe, with a smooth and waxy feel to the skin. The yellow, melting flesh is firm and without fiber and has a delicate, aromatic flavor. The fruit stores well at room temperature (70°F) for extended periods, and should not be refrigerated prior to ripening, as refrigeration alters the ripening and diminishes the eating quality. Dasheri is common throughout India; however, it is not a common export fruit, and is only occasionally available in the specialty markets of Europe. When it comes to eating quality, Dasheri is clearly among the world's elite; its exquisite, aromatic flesh is best appreciated when the fruit is eaten out of hand.

Tasting Notes: Gushing with tropical fruit scents, a silky raisin and black-currant concentrated flavor, and a lingering finish of lavender.

Diplomatico

Diplomatico was selected along the Pacific coast of Mexico. The fruit weigh from 10 to 14 ounces, with a striking crimson to red blush and a bright yellow background. Diplomatico has carved out a niche in the local markets due to its arresting color. The fruit are generally consumed ripe, when the flesh is dark orange, sweet, juicy, and melting. It has never been exported to any large extent, but at peak season in west Mexico, the Diplomatico is an important player in the local markets, and provides a fresh-mango experience to remember.

Tasting Notes: A rich, tangy aroma, with citrus, pineapple, and guava flavors.

East Indian

East Indian is a traditional juice mango selected in Jamaica but not well known away from the island. The fruit are oblong, with a smooth skin and a heavy wax coating. They weigh from 12 to 20 ounces and have are greenish- to bright-yellow skin, with a red blush on the shoulders, all overlaid by large white dots. The deep orange flesh is firm and juicy, with abundant coarse fiber throughout. The flavor is rich, aromatic, and spicy, but the fiber makes this mango difficult to eat out of hand. As a result, East Indian is usually used for fresh juices. These fruit are only rarely available in specialty stores in the United States or Europe, but they are common in markets throughout Jamaica and in other parts of the Caribbean.

Tasting Notes: Layers of clove, fresh thyme, and allspice emphasize the rich, distinctive tropical and coconut flavor notes.

Edward

Edward, a fine-quality dessert mango, is a hybrid of Haden Carabao. It was selected in the 1920s by Edward Simmonds of the U.S. Department of Agriculture Plant Introduction Garden in Miami, Florida. The fruit are oval to oblong, with an irregular, lightly waxed skin. They weigh from 16 to 24 ounces and are bright yellow at maturity. In optimum growing conditions, they can have a light red blush on the sun-exposed shoulder. The deep yellow flesh is without fiber, juicy and melting, with a sweet, rich, and spicy flavor. Though its yield is typically light, the superior flavor has encouraged commercial development in Peru and Israel. Production is often superior in arid climates like the equatorial desserts of Peru. Edward has gained in popularity due to its fine eating quality, and as consumers learn more about the range of mangos available, we may see greater interest in this fruit.

Tasting Notes: A zingy lemon-lime aroma, with a lavish mouthful of pineapple, tea, and cherry blossom flavors and a lingering peach taste.

15

Florigon

Florigon is thought to be the progeny of a Saigon seed planted in Ft. Lauderdale in the 1930s. The fruit are oval, with a smooth and lightly waxed skin. They weigh from 8 to 16 ounces and are bright yellow, only rarely with a hint of pink on the sun-exposed shoulder. The flesh is a deep yellow and without any fiber. It is soft, melting, and juicy, and excels as a frozen fruit. The flavor is rich and buttery, with a sweet and pleasant aroma. Florigon was primarily grown as a dooryard tree in South Florida due to its disease resistance and good eating quality; however, it has largely disappeared in recent years due to its low commercial viability. The fruit have been only of local importance, due to a thin skin and the resistance to yellow mangos in the marketplace.

Tasting Notes: A jazzy, sweet orange-blossom aroma with hints of cedar; the flavor fans out nicely, with apricot overtones.

Glenn

Glenn was discovered in the 1940s as a seedling at the residence of Roscoe E. Glenn in Miami, Florida. The fruit are oval to oblong and weigh from 16 to 20 ounces. They are bright yellow, with a pastel orange-red blush on the shoulder, overlaid by small yellow and white dots. The deep yellow flesh has no fiber and is soft and silky, with a rich, sweet, and aromatic flavor accompanied by a strong sweet aroma. Glenn is a favorite in the home gardens of Florida due to its consistent production, disease tolerance, and superb eating quality. It is grown in South America on a limited basis and imported into the United States, but it is not common. Its soft, melting flesh captivates South Floridians, who enjoy it out of hand. The local following has fueled its availability in local and roadside markets.

Tasting Notes: Loads of orange-blossom notes, with creamy and elegant apricot, nectar, and honey characteristics.

Golek

Golek was selected in Indonesia, where it is common in markets and home gardens. The fruit are oblong and elongated, with a lightly waxed, smooth skin. The fruit typically weigh from 4 to 8 ounces. The color is light green, often with a burnt-orange shoulder overlaid by small white dots. The flesh is a deep orange and is soft and juicy, with abundant fiber. It has a rich, spicy, and aromatic flavor. Golek is excluded from the export markets of the world, mostly due to their green color, small size, and high fiber content. This mango is, however, suited well for eating out of hand, for juices, and for ice creams.

Tasting Notes: A complex fragrance of orange marmalade, honey, and eucalyptus, with a spicy finish.

Haden

Haden was born of a Mulgoba seed planted in 1902 by Capt. F. O. Haden of Coconut Grove, Florida, and later cared for by his wife, Florence. It was the first fruiting of the Haden in 1910 that captivated the fledgling community of South Florida and inspired the creation of a large-scale mango industry. Haden fruit are oval and smooth, weighing from 24 to nearly 32 ounces. Their color is an exquisite bright yellow, with crimson and red highlights overlaid by a blanket of yellow and white dots. The flesh is firm, due to the moderate fiber, and the flavor of the Haden defines the mango for many in the tropics; it is rich, sweet, and aromatic with a mild, pleasant aroma. Haden dominated the mango industry of Florida for many years, and despite serious drawbacks to production, it remains a local favorite for home gardens. It is grown on a commercial scale in tropical climates around the world, and constitutes a considerable volume of the export mangos in the Western Hemisphere. Haden is important as a parent for new cultivars, both here in Florida, and beyond. Due to its disease susceptibility and production problems, many have foretold the demise of the Haden, yet it is still planted for commercial use due to its beauty and quality.

Tasting Notes: A distinct tropical aroma, with luscious peach and pineapple flavors and a snappy acidity.

Iris

Iris is a seedling of Irwin from the area around Delray Beach, Florida. Vigorous and productive, the tree is not commonly found outside home gardens in the South Florida area. Even here, you might have to search hard to find it. The fruit weigh from 12 to 16 ounces, and have a cylindrical, sigmoid shape. The color is a nearly complete crimson on the sun-exposed side, with considerable green on the shaded side. The flavor is sweet and quite a bit richer than that of Irwin. Iris fruits heavily, and the tree often requires thinning to produce larger fruit. The small fruit removed in thinning are well suited to pickling, or for achars and chutneys. Iris is one of many superior seedling mangos from South Florida with a fame that extends no farther than the property line of the home garden, or possibly even the county line.

Tasting Notes: Appealing lemon-lime and orange blossom notes, with plenty of green apple and pineapple flavors.

Israel 13-1

13-1 is a seedling of Turpentine that was selected in Israel. Within the small mango industry that has taken root in the arid production lands of Israel, it is used as a salt-tolerant rootstock for other mango cultivars. The fruit itself is small, ranging from 6 to 8 ounces. Greenish-yellow in color, it has a fibrous, juicy, dark orange pulp. Like Turpentine, it has a rich, sweet flavor, lending it to use in juices. Its small size, however, means it takes a considerable number to make enough juice to make the process worthwhile. Instead, perhaps it should instead be rolled on a table, the end bitten off, and the juice simply sucked out.

Tasting Notes: A rich floral and vanilla bean nose, with complex flavors of dark berry, cherry, and pineapple.

Israel BD 20-26

BD 20-26 is a numbered selection from the breeding program at Bet Dagan (hence, the BD), Israel. This selection has never been released to commercial cultivation, due to various limitations, but it has proven productive and of good quality in South Florida. The fruit are large, averaging from 20 to 28 ounces, with a yellow color overall, and a light pink to red blush when exposed to the sun. The flesh is yellow, firm, and without fiber, and the flavor is rich and sweet. This fruit is not currently available in commercial markets.

Tasting Notes: Mild, citrusy, appealing notes, with perky fruit flavors of pear, apple, and banana.

Israel BD 34-80

The name BD 34-80 designates a row and tree number in a seedling test block just outside Rehovot, Israel. This mango is one of a new generation of hybrids emerging from the few breeding programs throughout the world. It is ironic that such an ancient crop should be so new to organized breeding toward improvement in taste, storage, shipping, and disease resistance. With the mango, however, we have a wide palette of tastes, colors, aromas, and sizes to choose from, and this exciting program of breeding is just beginning to yield results.

Tasting Notes: Zingy citrus and green apple scents, with rounded flavors of peach, pear, and apricot.

Irwin

Irwin has been a perennial favorite for home gardens in South Florida, although it has fallen out of favor in recent years. It was selected in Miami in the 1940s for its beauty and productivity. The fruit weigh from 12 to 16 ounces and are produced at the beginning of the mango season. The fruit are bright yellow, with a dark crimson to red blush. The flavor is mild and sweet, and the flesh has no fiber. Irwin can be considered a "starter mango" in terms of flavor, which is to say that it will not offend anyone. The flavor is simply sweet and pleasant. It serves well in a home garden due to its manageability, productivity, and disease resistance. The Irwin is an integral component in Asian export markets due to the high-quality fruit grown in Taiwan.

Tasting Notes: An elegant citrus and blossom nose, with pretty flavors of peach, plum, and blackberry.

Ivory

The Ivory is from Thailand, where it is known by several different names. It is a middle-to-late-season mango in that country, and was historically an important export to China. The fruit are long and slender, and rather large in comparison to most commercially grown Thai mangos. The fruit weigh from 14 to 22 ounces and are bright yellow when ripe. The flesh is pale yellow and completely without fiber. Ivory can be used at the mature green stage, or when fully ripe, when its flavor is mild and sweet. This mango is not common within Thailand at present, as it is not as popular as some other cultivars. It does have considerable potential for export markets in the future.

Tasting Notes: A pleasant tropical nose, with a beautiful ripe-fruit taste of plum, caramelized pear, and vanilla bean.

Jakarta

The Jakarta was selected in Florida for its striking color and outstanding flavor. The fruit are large, averaging from 29 to 30 ounces, with an irregular and undulating skin. The skin is a stunning orange-red when exposed to the sun; yellow when ripened in shade. The flesh is a tender and juicy deep yellow, with rich and spicy flavor. The flavor of this mango is reminiscent of some of the best Caribbean cultivars. It ripens in the middle season and, unfortunately, is a poor bearer in many locations. Jakarta can sometimes be found in the smaller Caribbean islands, and is often found in cruise-line cuisine when local products are used. The flavor is quite strong and can be overpowering to some, although for a true mango lover, such a concept may be strange.

Tasting Notes: An exotic tropical aroma, with sweet, concentrated flavors of watermelon, banana, and coconut.

Jewel

Jewel is another selection from South Florida. The fruit are oval and rather small, from 10 to 16 ounces, but they have exceptional color, both when grown in the sun and in the interior canopy of the tree. The flesh is dark yellow, tender, and juicy, with a mild, sweet flavor. Jewel has never been grown commercially due to fruit-quality problems: internal softening or breakdown around the seed can cause "off" flavors. It is best used ripe, for fruit salads. Jewel is not presently available outside South Florida.

Tasting Notes: A lively tropical blossom-perfumed nose, with abundant peach and pineapple flavors.

Julie

Julie is a traditional dessert cultivar in Jamaica, widely grown on the island, but not well known beyond its shores. The fruit have a flattened, oval shape and an irregular skin surface with a light waxy coating. The fruit are small, weighing around 8 ounces. When ripe, they are green to burnt orange in color, with a red blush on the sun-exposed shoulder. The orange flesh is juicy and completely without fiber, with a deep, rich, and spicy flavor. Julie should be eaten as quickly as possible after ripening, since its quality declines rapidly. The fruit should be protected from cold temperatures during ripening. Due to the irregular cropping habit of the tree and the lack of large commercial orchards, Julie has never been readily available to the export market. In recent years, however, there has been an effort to increase its supply to meet the demands of ethnic markets in Europe and the United States.

Tasting Notes: Spicy notes of clove and cinnamon, with hints of coconut and lavish flavors of fig, caramel, and raisin.

Keitt

Keitt was discovered as a seedling tree on the property of Mrs. J. N. Keitt of Homestead, Florida, in the 1940s. The fruit are oval and quite large, weighing from 24 to 40 ounces. In commercial terms, Keitt is considered a green mango because it often retains a green skin color when fully ripe and ready to eat, with only a slight pink blush. In some locations, however, it can develop a light yellow color with a strong pink or red blush. The flesh is without fiber, lemon yellow, firm, and juicy. Keitt has a mild and sweet flavor with pleasant aromatic overtones. It dominates the Western export market for late mangos, because its season is a full month or more later than most commercial cultivars. Among the heaviest bearing of cultivars and highly adaptable to many climates, Keitt is a favorite in Asian cultures for consumption at the mature-green stage or for pickles. The fruit are tolerant of disease and rough handling, making this mango perfect for commercial cultivation.

Tasting Notes: Interesting layers of coconut, berry, and lime notes, with creamy vanilla and lush peach flavors.

Kensington

Kensington is the major cultivar of Australia, to the extent that it has largely excluded all other cultivars from cultivation. The fruit are ovate, with a smooth, lightly waxed skin. The color is yellow, with a red blush on the sun-exposed shoulders. It weighs from 12 to 20 ounces. The lemon-yellow flesh is soft, juicy, and completely without fiber. It has a sweet, aromatic and distinctive flavor. Within Australia, the "Kensington flavor" is greatly desired and fuels a dependence on this cultivar. This mango is exported from Australia to the markets of Asia, but is not commonly found in Europe or the United States. It is generally consumed out of hand.

Tasting Notes: Remarkably fresh citrus notes, with flavors of ripe peach, banana, and sweet grapefruit.

Kent

Kent was selected as a seedling tree on the property of Leith D. Kent, Coconut Grove, Florida, in the 1940s. The fruit are oval, with a smooth and waxy skin, and weigh from 24 to 32 ounces. The fruit ripen to a golden yellow, with a deep red or crimson blush overlaid by numerous small yellow dots. In arid climates, however, Kent retains its green color even when fully ripe. The deep orange flesh is soft, melting, and juicy, with an exceptionally rich, sweet flavor. Kent is imported to the United States from South and Central America and is considered by many to have the best eating quality of all commercially available mango cultivars. Unfortunately, its soft flesh suffers considerable damage in transport and display. Besides being a fine dessert mango, Kent is also well suited for juicing and drying.

Tasting Notes: A vibrant, musky and tropical floral nose, with cherry blossom, ripe fruit, and caramel flavors.

Kyo Savoy

Kyo Savoy was selected in Thailand and sets the standard of quality for the mature green mango. The fruit command a premium price in local markets and are served sliced, with a variety of dipping sauces. The fruit are sigmoid, long, and slender, with a bluntly pointed apex. They weigh from 14 to 18 ounces, with a smooth and lightly waxy skin. When mature, the fruit are a dark green, with no blush or prominent dots, making them easy to distinguish from other mangos. The flesh is firm and crisp, with considerable juiciness and texture. The flesh is sweet, with an acidic bite. If allowed, the fruit will ripen to a light yellow, when the flesh softens and develops a sweet and silky flavor. As with other mature green mangos, texture is vital to quality: The flesh should be firm and crunchy. As the fruit lose water, they develop rubbery flesh, discouraging their export to distant markets.

Tasting Notes: A zingy citrus nose evoking flavors of green apple, ginger, and toasted macadamia nut.

Madame Francis

Madame Francis comes from Haiti, where it has been a traditional dessert cultivar for decades. The fruit are oblong and sigmoid in shape, with an undulating skin surface and a lightly waxed skin. Their size ranges from 16 to 20 ounces, and their color from greenish to bright yellow, without any blush. The dark orange flesh is soft and juicy, with a rich, spicy, and sweet flavor. Madame Francis is one of the few specialty mangos that has been available in the United States for a number of years. Its eating quality is considered superior to other commercially-available mangos, although the fiber can be excessive in some fruit. Most of the fruit are harvested and collected from small farmers in Haiti, and there have been considerable problems with quality consistency. Since consumers outside of specialty markets are unfamiliar with Madame Francis, its importance in export markets has unfortunately remained limited.

Tasting Notes: Hints of anise and cinnamon, with generous flavors of caramel, fig, and candied orange peel.

Mallika

Mallika is a hybrid of Neelum and Dasheri, and is considered one of the best of the new generation of Indian dessert mangos. The tree is semi-dwarf, making it attractive to mango growers outside of India—always looking for new mangos for the niche markets around the world. The bright yellow fruit have a flattened, oblong shape, with a rounded base and an irregular non-waxy skin. They weigh from 10 to 18 ounces. When properly ripened, the firm but completely fiber-free flesh is deep orange, with an intensely sweet, rich, and highly aromatic flavor. Mallika fruit are harvested mature and green, before they "break color" on the tree. For ripening they should be stored at a temperature of not less than 70°F for 2 to 3 weeks. The fruit may be refrigerated after it is completely ripe. Although best consumed as a fresh mango, Mallika is also excellent for juicing and drying.

Tasting Notes: An exotic aroma of papaya, tropical flowers, and musk with layers of prune and fig flavors.

Manila

Manila was selected in Mexico as a seedling grown from a seed from the Philippines. The fruit are long, slender, and sigmoid, with a smooth, lightly waxy skin. The fruit weigh from 8 to 12 ounces and are orangish-yellow, with a slight pink blush on the shoulder exposed to the sun. The deep-yellow flesh is soft and juicy and completely without fiber, with a sweet and aromatic flavor. Traditionally, Manila was grown from seed throughout Mexico, which resulted in many variants in color, size, flavor, and yield. Today, many Manila variants are recognized in Mexico, though they are usually restricted to specific regions. Manila has set a standard for excellence in eating quality in Mexico, and has been widely used for canning. Its Indochinese heritage is evident in flavor and flesh characteristics, making it a good candidate for ethnic markets; however, the thin, tender skin has limited its export as a fresh fruit.

Tasting Notes: Spicy notes of orange and lime zest give way to flavors of honey, raisin, and hazelnut.

Manzanillo

Manzanillo was selected in West Mexico, and has been a local favorite in the region for decades. The fruit are oblong to blocky in shape, with a dark red blush that covers nearly the entire fruit. At first glance, Manzanillo looks like Kent, although it tends to be more irregular. The fruit range from 14 to 20 ounces and appear toward the end of the fruiting season. The flesh is dark orange, with little fiber and a rich, sweet flavor. At present, Manzanillo is not exported fresh to any large extent, and is not likely to be found in U.S. grocery stores. Due to its superior flesh quality and color, the fruit has been used for drying, and organic dried Manzanillo slices can be found in U.S. markets. Though not widely available, its excellent quality when properly ripened warrants further attention and development in Mexico and beyond.

Tasting Notes: A crisp green apple nose, revealing tastes of citrus, red grape, and pineapple.

Mulgoba

Mulgoba was the first superior-quality grafted mango to fruit in Florida in 1898. The tree was imported from India in 1889 by the U.S. Department of Agriculture and grown on the property of Elbridge Gale near Lake Worth. The fruit are oval, with a smooth skin, and weigh from 10 to 14 ounces. The skin is bright yellow, with a pink or red blush overlaid by many small white dots. The lemon-yellow flesh is soft, tender, melting, and juicy, with a rich, spicy, and sweet flavor and a strong, pleasant aroma. There is some fiber in the flesh, although it is generally not offensive. Interestingly, there is no evidence of a mango fitting the description of Mulgoba in India. What we call Mulgoba may instead have been a root sprout arising from the original tree following a severe freeze. Regardless of its origin, Mulgoba was the first exceptional mango with color to fruit in Florida. Due to its disease susceptibility, poor yield and soft, easily damaged skin, it is no longer grown in Florida or other western areas, but some of its positive traits persist in its offspring, Haden.

Tasting Notes: A snappy allspice and citrus-blossom aroma, with layers of ripe melon, tangerine, and citron.

Naomi

Naomi is a newly-named cultivar from the recent breeding program in Israel. The fruit are large, averaging from 20 to 24 ounces, and particularly beautiful, with a bright yellow background and a bright red blush. The flesh is soft, without fiber, and extremely juicy. The color is dark yellow to almost orange, and the flavor is mild and sweet. Naomi was released a few years ago, but has never attained a position of prominence either in or outside of Israel. It is one of the many interesting cultivars coming from modern breeding programs. We will have to wait and see which ones, if any, make the grade in the world mango trade. For now, Naomi remains a quality mango well suited to eating ripe.

Tasting Notes: A vibrant floral aroma, with flavors reminiscent of sweet white peaches, pears, and lemon zest.

Neelum

Neelum is a South Indian dessert mango, widely grown in India and China. The fruit weigh 9 ounces, and have an ovate-oblique shape. They are smooth skinned and bright yellow on ripening, with no blush. The flesh is without fiber and has a rich, aromatic flavor that is overpowering to some palates. Neelum is best suited for fresh consumption, or for slices or cubes, since the firm flesh holds its shape well when cut. The fruit have a late ripening season and can be stored for an extended time, offering advantages in marketing. This mango, however, is only occasionally exported outside of its production areas, due to the significant local demand. Neelum is a dwarf tree and may fit into modern production systems, which could increase its availability in commercial export markets.

Tasting Notes: A complex aroma of clove and cinnamon, with full flavors of ripe red berries, plums, and apricots.

Nam Doc Mai

Nam Doc Mai, or "nectar of flowers," is among the best-known dessert mangos of Thailand, with an exceptional appearance and eating quality. It can sometimes be found in specialty markets in Japan, Europe, and the United States. In Thailand, there are many recognized strains of Nam Doc Mai, which are classified according to the uses for the fruit. The fruit are long, slender, and sigmoid, weighing from 12 to 16 ounces. When ripe, they range from greenish- to canary-yellow, only rarely with a reddish blush on the sun-exposed shoulder. The fruit are most often eaten when ripe, when the flesh is soft and juicy with a sweet and aromatic flavor. In Thailand and throughout much of Asia, this cultivar epitomizes a ripe dessert fruit, with a smooth, silky texture and extreme sweetness and bouquet. The fruit are also used while mature green for dipping in sauces and for making preserves and pickles.

Tasting Notes: Green: A zingy citrus and lemon-blossom nose, with crisp green apple, grapefruit, and sour cherry flavors. Ripe: Graceful hints of anise and cinnamon, with loads of complex flavors of melon, peach, and tangerine.

Number 11

Number 11 probably originated in Jamaica over a century ago. It was sent to Florida in the 1860s, where it was widely distributed. At the onset of mango development in the region, Number 11 became one of the most common mangos grown in the Caribbean. Trees were grown from seed, resulting in considerable variation and many recognized strains. The shape is ovate, with an irregular skin surface. The fruit are small, weighing from 4 to 8 ounces. Even when ripe, the skin color can remain green, with a slight orange-red blush. The flesh is lemon yellow and firm, with abundant fiber that makes the fruit difficult to eat. They are often softened by beating against a hard surface and squeezing the juice out. Number 11, though rarely marketed commercially, is found in rural markets and roadside stands.

Tasting Notes: Floral notes of honey and clove, gushing with tropical pineapple, grapefruit, and guava flavors.

Okrong Tong

Okrong Tong, a Thai dessert mango, is most often eaten ripe, when the fruit are a golden yellow and the flesh soft, juicy, and delicious. It is common in most fruit markets within Thailand, but uncommon outside of the region. The fruit are oblong, long, and slender, often with a slight sigmoid shape. They are small, usually weighing from 6 to 8 ounces, and turn from deep green to golden yellow on ripening. The skin is pebbly and irregular to the touch, while the flesh is melting and juicy, often with significant fiber. When ripe, the flavor is distinctive, with an intense sweetness accompanied by a slight acidity. During much of the mango season in Thailand, Okrong Tong dominates the local fruit market, and is eaten out of hand on the street. Due to its size, shape, and fiber content, the fruit are often squeezed from the skin directly into the mouth, and the skin and pit discarded. The distinctive, rich flavor of Okrong Tong lends it to juicing and use in tropical desserts.

Tasting Notes: A gentle aroma of ginger and mint, with appealing velvety pineapple, melon, and banana flavors.

Oro

Oro is from West Mexico, where it is one of the most popular market mangos. In fact, during the region's early fruiting season it dominates markets to the exclusion of other cultivars. The fruit range from 14 to 22 ounces in size, with an oblong, sigmoid shape. The color is a less-than-spectacular greenish-yellow with a dull red blush on the sun-exposed shoulder. The flesh is firm and a little rubbery, with a mild flavor when fully ripe. The major use of Oro, however, is as a mature green fruit to be sliced and eaten raw with salt and chili. Outside of local markets, the Oro is uncommon, and if found, is not identified by name.

Tasting Notes: A spice-laced nose of clove and cinnamon, with powerful flavors of vanilla, fig, and caramel.

Osteen

Osteen was selected on Merritt Island, Florida, in the 1940s as a potential commercial mango for Florida. It never caught on commercially in the state, but continues to attract attention from international mango growers. The fruit are oblong and large, averaging from 18 to 27 ounces. The background color of the skin is yellow, with a crimson or sometimes lavender blush—distinctive among mango cultivars. Osteen has excellent flesh quality: firm and juicy, with a lemon-yellow color. The flavor is mild and sweet, and there is little fiber in the flesh. It is not currently important as a commercial mango, but export markets have shown growing interest in this cultivar, particularly in Australia and South Africa.

Tasting Notes: A pleasant aromatic scent of green grapes, balanced with pear and passion fruit flavors.

Palmer

Palmer is one of the best-colored mango selections from Florida. The fruit are oblong and rather large, ranging from 18 to 30 ounces. The skin color, a complete purple or red while developing, turns a light red and yellow when ripe. The flesh is firm and melting, while the flavor is mild and sweet, and in some years can be quite rich. Palmer is a late-season fruit, ripening after Tommy Atkins and before Keitt. When fully ripe it is great for eating out of hand, and also for drying. Palmer grows in tropical climates throughout the Western Hemisphere, and can be found in some national markets within Latin America, and occasionally in the export market. In some years, Brazil exports Palmer to the United States. The fruit offers commercial challenges, primarily due to the difficulty in judging its maturity: deceivingly, it turns red early in its development and if picked too early, won't ripen at all.

Tasting Notes: Pleasant notes of fruit and spice, with flavors suggesting roasted pears, apples, and nuts.

Prieto

Prieto is an heirloom cultivar from Cuba, an island rich in mango diversity. The fruit are small in size, ranging from 8 to 10 ounces. The skin can be so dark a green that it appears black, prompting its name, Spanish for "black." Within this dark exterior lies a deep-orange flesh with considerable fiber. If the fruit is rolled on a table to release the juice for drinking, however, a rich, sweet, and spicy flavor will be the reward. Prieto is not exported and is not commonly planted for commercial use today. In Cuba, however, it remains an important market mango.

Tasting Notes: A deep floral aroma, with a pleasurable balance of pineapple, peach, and candied-orange-peel flavors.

Rad

Rad, also called Rat or Phimsen Mun, is a versatile Thai mango used at the mature green stage and also as a ripe fruit. The fruit are long, slender, and sigmoid, often with a hooked projection at the top, and average from 12 to 16 ounces. The apex of the fruit is blunter than that of Nam Doc Mai. Rad is a uniform light green at the mature green stage, turning to a light yellow on ripening. The flavor when mature green is slightly acid, yet with an aromatic, sweet base. The texture, which is key in the consumption of mature green mangos, is crispy and juicy, like a Granny Smith apple. When ripe, it has a melting flesh with a sweet and aromatic flavor. Rad is not common outside of Thailand, but can sometimes be found in Chinese or Japanese specialty markets. In Asia, it is prized for eating with spicy and salty dipping sauces. Care must be taken that the fruit do not lose moisture prior to consumption, as this will affect the quality of their texture.

Tasting Notes: Remarkable fresh notes of banana, tea, and pine, with the acidity of green apple and sour cherry.

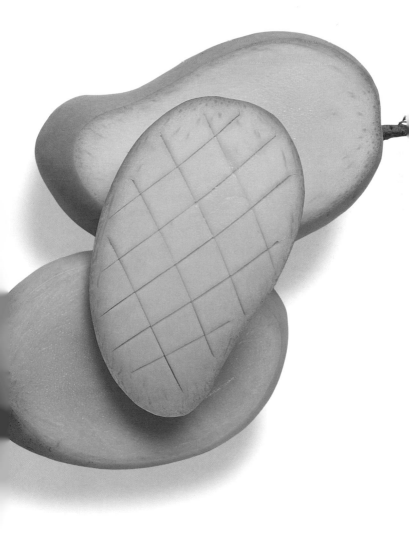

Rosa

A traditional cultivar from Brazil, Rosa probably originated in Goa, India. Early Portuguese settlers brought the seed that led to its development. The fruit are sigmoid, oblong, and ovate, and weigh from 14 to 18 ounces. The skin color is a striking pastel pink and red, unique among mangos cultivars. The flesh is deep yellow to orange, with considerable fiber. Due to its fiber, Rosa has typically been used to make juices in Brazil. The flavor is rich and spicy, reminiscent of the finest dessert mangos of India. This powerful, sweet aroma epitomizes the true essence of mango. There have been limited exports of this mango from South America to the United States, but it remains rare in U.S. markets. For the people of Brazil, however, Rosa remains important in local markets.

Tasting Notes: Flamboyant notes of cinnamon, allspice, and clove, gushing with flavors of pear, peach, and passion fruit.

Ruby

Ruby, yet another selection from Miami, is oblong and quite small, ranging from 7 to 11 ounces. In heavy crop years, the size can be even smaller. The background skin color is yellow, with a bright red blush, particularly when exposed to the sun. The flesh is firm and juicy and has a fine fiber that is not objectionable. The flavor is rich, aromatic, and spicy. A middle to late-season cultivar in Florida, Ruby can be found in South American domestic markets from time to time, especially in Southern Brazil and northern Colombia. The fruit are consumed when completely ripe, and are well suited for fruit salads and eating out of hand.

Tasting Notes: An elegant orange blossom aroma, with flavors reminiscent of cherry, peach, and hazelnut.

Sabre

Sabre originated in Africa, where it was probably introduced by Portuguese explorers and settlers in the 1700s. The historical roots of this mango are anchored firmly in southern India and Goa, and its fruit is characteristic of many of the mangos from that region. Long and slender, these mangos have a characteristic sigmoid shape. They are bright red to crimson on the side exposed to the sun, and predominantly yellow on the shaded surface. The fruit range from 14 to 18 ounces. The rich, sweet, and spicy flesh is dark orange, with considerable coarse fiber throughout. Its color and flavor make this a superior mango. Major uses of Sabre are for eating out of hand and juicing; Sabre is also used as a rootstock for the grafting of other cultivars in Africa and elsewhere in the world.

Tasting Notes: Luscious aromatic notes of vanilla, clove, and toffee, with generous flavors of fig, raisin, and honey.

Sandersha

Sandersha is a traditional Indian cultivar selected for use in processed mango products, both in its mature-green and ripe stages. The large fruit reach weights of 24 to 32 ounces, and are oblong and sigmoid, with a smooth skin and light wax covering. When ripe, they are light green to light yellow, with a pink blush on the sun-exposed shoulder overlaid by many large russet dots. The lemon-yellow flesh is firm and rather dry, with abundant fine fiber throughout. Sandersha lacks sweetness, and instead has a spicy flavor. Although not suited for fresh consumption, Sandersha is among the best mangos for making achar, chutney, and other preserves. The firm flesh holds its shape during heating and canning, resulting in a superior texture, and the slight acidity adds flavor to cooked dishes. Sandersha and other processing cultivars are common in India and Pakistan, but are not available in commercial markets in the Western Hemisphere. The Florida cultivar Keitt, which is available in these markets, is a good substitute.

Tasting Notes: Complex aromas of violet, anise, and black pepper, with earthy flavors of green olive, artichoke, and almond.

Toledo

Toledo, an heirloom cultivar from western Cuba, is common in markets all across the island. The fruit are small, averaging less than 6 ounces. The skin is speckled greenish-yellow, with a slight orange-pink blush. The flesh is fibrous, but the flavor is rich and sweet. Toledo typifies the Caribbean mango, abundant in season and highly flavorful. Toledo will never replace Tommy Atkins in the export market, but should always have a place in the lowland Caribbean.

Tasting Notes: A concentrated fruit and spice nose, with loads of ripe peach and nectarine flavors.

Tommy Atkins

Tommy Atkins was discovered as a seedling tree in the 1940s in Broward County, Florida. Its stunning color, heavy production, and disease tolerance attracted the attention of commercial mango growers in the area. The fruit are oval to oblong, with a smooth, waxy skin, and weigh from 16 to 24 ounces. The fruit is orange-yellow, with a crimson or dark red blush often covering most of the skin. The flesh has a fine fiber throughout, which gives it a firm texture. It is lemon to deep yellow, with a mild and sweet flavor. Many consider its eating quality to be only fair, although quality depends greatly on the conditions under which the fruit are produced. Due to its poor flavor, Tommy Atkins was rejected for commercial production in Florida for many years. However, its other attributes, including color, disease tolerance, high yield, and the tough nature of the tree and fruit eventually outweighed this negative. Tommy Atkins has gone on to dominate commercial export production in Florida and the Western Hemisphere. Today, it constitutes the majority of the mangos imported into the United States. Given its limitations of flavor and worse, its all-too-often off-flavor (resulting from softening and decay around the seed), the world searches for its replacement. Meanwhile, Tommy Atkins remains king.

Tasting Notes: Appealing fruity, aromatic notes of orange blossom, with flavors of pineapple, peach, and tangerine.

Tong Dam

Tong Dam is an older, multipurpose Thai cultivar suited both for use at the mature green stage, and when fully ripe. The fruit are often sold at street stands with decorative cuts to demonstrate the alluring contrast between the drab, dark green skin and the deep golden flesh. The name translates to "black gold," which is most fitting. The fruit weigh from 14 to 18 ounces, and have a characteristicly long, slender, and bluntly pointed shape. Tong Dam ripens early in the season and is usually marketed in Thailand before the Nam Doc Mai and Okrong Tong season begins. The fruit are best eaten while the flesh is still firm, since the flavor becomes bland when it is fully ripe. This mango is uncommon outside of Thailand, although it may occasionally be encountered in some Southeast Asian specialty markets.

Tasting Notes: A refined, mildly sweet fruit aroma, brimming with creamy citrus and pineapple flavors.

Turpentine

Turpentine describes a group of similar mango selections common throughout the tropical regions of the world. Turpentine was first recognized in South Florida in the 1880s in the area of Coconut Grove, Florida. The fruit are oval, with a smooth, waxy skin. They are produced in clusters and are small, averaging from 4 to 8 ounces. The skin is bright yellow, only rarely with a pink blush on the sun-exposed shoulder. The deep yellow flesh is firm and juicy, and the flavor is rich, spicy, and aromatic. The abundant coarse fiber generally requires that the fruit be beaten or rolled on a hard surface and the juice then squeezed out. The deep, rich flavor of this fruit makes it well-suited for juices and frozen desserts, although the fiber makes processing difficult. This mango was traditionally used as a rootstock for the grafting of other cultivars, and it remains important for this use to the present day. Turpentines are not typically sold in modern supermarkets, although they can be found at reasonable prices in the markets of tropical America.

Tasting Notes: An exotic aroma of chamomile, cinnamon, and clove, giving way to concentrated melon, nectarine, and plum flavors.

Valencia Pride

Valencia Pride is another of the high-quality seedlings from South Florida selected in the late 1940s. It is long and slender, with a slight sigmoid shape. The fruit are large, weighing from 20 to 30 ounces, and are bright yellow with a crimson to red blush over the sun-exposed portion of the fruit. The flesh is firm but melting, with a deep yellow color. The flavor is sweet, but mild and pleasant to most who sample it. Valencia Pride can occasionally be found in specialty markets, although it is uncommon outside South Florida. It is best used when ripe and is a favorite in late summer, after the glut of mid-season cultivars. Valencia Pride has always possessed considerable commercial potential, but has yet to be produced on a large scale.

Tasting Notes: A zingy citrus and orange-blossom bouquet, with beautiful flavors of orange, ripe peach, and candied almond.

Vallenato

Vallenato is a traditional cultivar from the north coast of Colombia. It has often been called Manzano ("apple,") in the region due to its deep red color and round shape. The fruit are actually oval, with an average size of 9 to 12 ounces. The skin is smooth and waxy, with a deep red color covering nearly the entire surface. When ripe, the red blush of the fruit brightens to give a most striking appearance. Due to a fine fiber throughout, the flesh is quite firm, but the fiber is not objectionable. The flesh is juicy and sweet, with a rich aromatic flavor. The fruit can be stored for many days at room temperature, while still retaining its exceptional flavor. The Vallenato sees limited extent from Colombia, but is difficult to locate outside the north coast of South America. Vallenato has the characteristics needed to become a successful export item, but its small size has been a serious deterrent.

Tasting Notes: Racy notes of jasmine and orange blossom, layered with luscious berry, tangerine, and apricot flavors.

Van Dyke

Van Dyke is one of the many quality mango seedlings selected in South Florida in the 1950s and 1960s. The fruit are small, averaging between 10 and 16 ounces, with a striking crimson and red blush overlaying a bright yellow background. Adding to its appeal are the many white dots that give Van Dyke its distinctive beauty. The flesh is firm, deep yellow orange, with a rich, sweet, and spicy flavor. A fine, unobjectionable fiber throughout the flesh adds to its firmness, and suits the fruit for use in salads and wherever holding of shape is important. Due to some limitations in storage and handling, Van Dyke is not common, but is found off and on throughout the year in commercial grocery stores in the United States and Europe.

Tasting Notes: A graceful nose of honeysuckle and lilac, with flavors of pineapple, tangerine, and honey.

Zill

Zill was selected by Lawrence Zill from a residence in Lake Worth, Florida in the 1930s. The fruit are oval to ovate, with irregular and heavily waxed skin. They are small in size, from 8 to 12 ounces. The ripe fruit are greenish-yellow to yellow, with a dark red or crimson blush overlaid with many small white dots. The flesh is pale yellow, quite soft and juicy, with no fiber. The flavor is rich, sweet, and spicy, with a strong and pleasant aroma. Due to its production, appearance, and eating quality, Zill was one of the first Florida mangos to gain importance around the world. It has decreased in popularity, however, due to its soft flesh, small size, and poor storage traits. Yet the rich, exceptional flavor of Zill has made this fruit a favorite among ethnic Indian consumers in niche markets in the United States (traditional Indian cultivars are unavailable here). Besides its ethnic appeal, Zill is one of the preferred mangos for dehydrating, due to its unique flavor and deep orange color.

Tasting Notes: A rich aroma of dried fruit with hints of lavender, and loads of ripe peach and nectarine flavors.

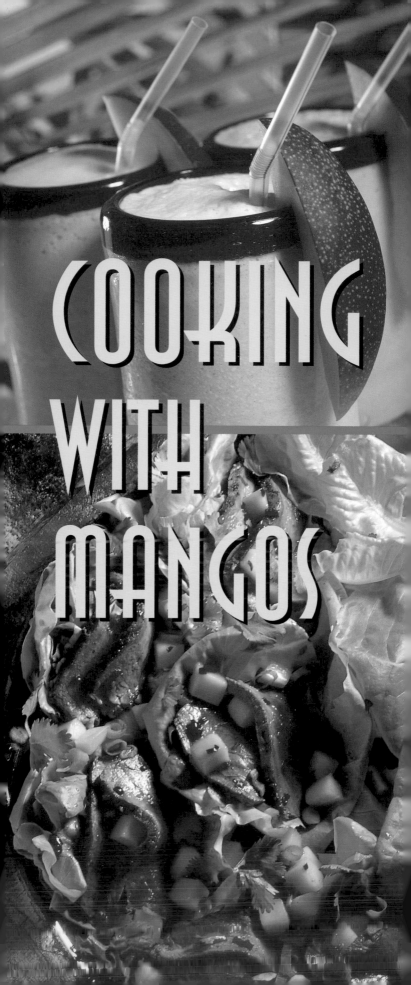

COOKING
WITH
MANGOS

Selecting and Storing Mangos

In the world of mangos, there are two main kinds: green and ripe. Both are delicious, but they have very different uses. *Green mangos* refer to young fruit, usually pale green, without a hint of color; crisp, with a sour taste, although sometimes sweet and sour.

There are two categories of green mangos: immature and mature. The *immature green mango* is a fruit that is picked early from the tree, therefore it will never become ripe and sweet. Immature green mangos are often used in their entirety—the skin, flesh and soft stone are all edible—most commonly for pickles and chutneys. A note of caution though: some people are sensitive to the sap under the skin of these immature mangos, and develop a rash very similar to poison ivy (a species cousin of the mango).

The *mature green mango* is grown to full maturity on the tree before being harvested. The skin of the mango becomes thick, tough and inedible; its flesh firm, and fiber content less apparent. The mature green fruit is similar in flavor and texture to a freshly picked crisp, tart green apple. The stone in the mature green mango develops a hard shell to protect the seedling inside.

When selecting green mangos, look for an unblemished skin of dull, bluish-green or muted colors, and very firm flesh. If you want to store the mango for any extended period and delay the ripening process, mature green mangos can be kept at 55 degrees, without damage, for two weeks.

Ripe mangos are harvested when their skin grows yellow to orange and blushed and their flesh is firm. Although they are not completely ripened, most mangos sold in fruit stands and groceries are considered ripe. Ripening the fruit off the tree allows it to ripen more evenly and develop a better flavor. As the mango sweetens, its skin color usually becomes more spectacular. Pale greens turn to sunset yellows, blush pinks to deep purples; multi-colors turn striking red blush and crimson with bright yellow backgrounds.

The flesh of a ripe mango is usually yellow-orange in color, though it can range greatly in hue and intensity. Fiber content plays an important role in ripe mangos. Most Indian and Southeast Asian varieties have very little fiber compared to the Caribbean, Latin, and Florida varieties. Little or no fiber makes the fruit more custard-like in texture. Because of their texture, slightly more fibrous mangos usually have more bite and mouth appeal.

When selecting a mango from the fruit stand, first look for a firm, unblemished skin, usually with bright colors. Knowing when and how you wish to use the mango will help you select and identify the proper fruit. If you want a sweet, ripe mango to be used that day, lead with your nose. Smell for a sweet, tropical ambrosial scent coming from the stem end. Then give it a light but firm squeeze. The flesh should have some give, like a ripe banana, but your fingers should not leave an imprint.

On the other hand, when purchasing mangos for later use, buy a firmer-fleshed mango with tight skin, whose color may still be a little dull. To ripen this fruit, keep it at room temperature (about 70 degrees) open to the air for several days. Avoid refrigeration during the ripening process; mangos may be chilled before eating if desired.

The ripe mango is prefect for eating when the skin has come to full bright color tones, its flesh is soft to the squeeze, and its sweet aroma fills the house with a lush tropical scent.

Fully ripened fruit can be stored in the refrigerator at 40 to 45 degrees for up to one week.

Clockwise: Allen, Deanna, and Liza Susser

Cutting Mangos

Sometimes the best way to enjoy a ripe mango is to roll up your sleeves and just dig your teeth into it. But when you're preparing a mango for cooking, follow these simple steps to cutting.

1) Turn the mango on one of its narrow sides so the fleshy cheek can be sliced off. Using a sharp knife, cut through the cheek, about one-third of the way into the mango.

2) Cut all the way through, letting the cheek separate from the fruit. Repeat the process on the other cheek.

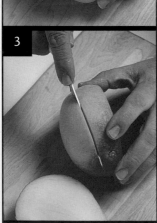

3) Cut the remaining wedges from the stone and use along with the cheeks as called for in the recipe: whole, cut into wedges, slices, dice, or cubes. (To those unwilling to let any mango go to waste, the author recommends sucking any remaining flesh from the stone.)

How to Hedgehog a Mango

Once you've removed both cheeks (described at left), insert the point of the knife into the flesh of one cheek.

1) Carefully, without cutting through the skin, slice only just deep enough to touch the skin. Slice short lines along the inside of the flesh. Continue to cut 5 or 6 lines in the same direction equidistant from each other.

2) Using the point of the knife, cut 5 or 6 lines in the opposite direction to the first set of cuts—perpendicularly for cube shapes, or diagonally for diamond shapes as shown in figure 2.

3) Now, holding the mango cheek in both hands with your thumbs and palms on top of the fruit, gently push upwards from below with your fingers. Apply pressure to the center first.

4) Continue to gently ease the remaining flesh upwards until you have the skin pressed inside out and the flesh pops out in a hedgehog design.

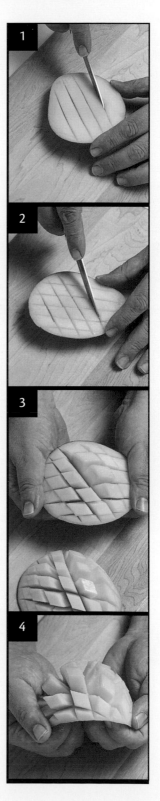

Recipes

BEVERAGES AND STARTERS

Chef Allen's Mango Martini 70

Mango Daiquiri 70

Mango Lassi 71

Mango Frappé 71

Lobster and Mango Salad 72

Mango Souscaille with Prosciutto 73

Shrimp and Mango Curry 74

Thai Steak and Mango Salad 77

Spiced-Rubbed Jumbo Scallops
  with Mango Salsa 78

Mango-Shrimp Cocktail 79

Crab and Mango Salad 80

Tuna and Mango Sashimi Salad 83

Mango-Braised Drumsticks 84

Mango and Avocado Salad 85

MAIN DISHES

Grilled Mahimahi with Mango Sauce
  and Mango-Shrimp Salsa 88

Seared Herb-Coated Tuna
  with Saffron-Macadamia-Mango Rice 90

Lamb Chops with Dried Mango and Ginger 92

Creole Fried Chicken with Mango 94

Panfried Soft-Shell Crabs
  with Green Mango Slaw 95

Ale-Roasted Pompano
  with Mango-Cashew Salsa 96

Roast Pork Loin with Mango Mojo
  and Yellow Plantains 99

Chicken and Green Mango Stew 100

Pan-Roasted Lobster with Spicy Mango Glaze ... 101

CONDIMENTS

Hot and Sour Mango Relish 104

Raw-Mango Chutney 105

Quick Ripe-Mango Chutney 106

Green Mango Chutney 107

Mango Vinaigrette 108

Mango Mojo 109

Green Mango Pickle (Achaar) 110

Green Mango Slaw 111

Mango and Papaya Salsa 112

Dried-Fruit Chutney 113

Mango Chow 114

Mango Jam 115

Mango-Peach Marmalade 116

Mango Ketchup 117

DESSERTS

Mango, Banana, and Pistachio Strudel 120

Mango Sour Cream Crumb Cake 121

Ginger-Rum Grilled Pineapple
   with Mango Sorbet 122

Country Mango Tarts 125

Mango and Almond Macaroon Tart 126

Mango Cobbler 127

Indian Mango Ice Cream 128

Mangos with Sticky Rice 129

Mango Split with Rum-Caramel Sauce
   and Macadamia Nuts 130

Mango Crème Brûlée
   with Lavender-Nut Fricassee 132

Mango Leather 133

Mango Gingersnaps 134

Mango Cheesecake 135

BEVERAGES

AND STARTERS

Preceding page: Mango Frappé (recipe opposite) and Lobster and Mango Salad (recipe on page 72)

Chef Allen's Mango Martini

At Chef Allen's, July is Mango Madness month. We start by macerating hundreds of pounds of mangos in gallons of vodka, so we can put them up for the winter. We never want to let go of those bright, summer flavors. Use ripe mangos that have the sweet aroma of the tropics.

Serves 2

> **Ice cubes**
> **1 cup Mango Vodka (recipe follows)**
> **2 twists of lime zest**

Put the ice cubes in a shaker glass. Pour the vodka over the ice cubes and shake well. Strain into 2 well-chilled Martini glasses. Garnish each drink with a lime twist.

Mango Vodka: Peel 3 ripe mangos, cut the flesh from the pit, and cut into large dice. Put the mangos in a clean 1-quart mason jar. Add 2 cups vodka and seal the jar. Let sit in a cool, dark place for 2 to 3 days before using. Store leftover vodka up to 5 days. Makes 2 cups.

Mango Daiquiri

Ernest Hemingway probably enjoyed mango daiquiris during his days in Cuba, a country known for its high-quality rum and flavorful mangos.

Serves 2

> **1 scoop crushed ice**
> **1/4 large ripe mango, peeled, cut from the pit, and diced**
> **2 tablespoons freshly squeezed juice of key lime, or Persian lime**
> **1 teaspoon superfine sugar**
> **1/2 cup dark rum**

In a blender, combine all the ingredients and purée until smooth. Serve in daiquiri glasses.

Mango Lassi

An Indian favorite, lassi is a yogurt drink. It's a great light snack in the summer. Depending on the sweetness of the mango, you may not need sugar.

Serves 2

1 1/4 cups plain yogurt
1 ripe mango, peeled, cut from the pit, and diced
10 ice cubes
1 tablespoon superfine sugar (optional)

In a blender, combine the yogurt, mango, and ice cubes. Blend until smooth. Taste and add sugar, if desired, and blend again. Serve in tall, chilled glasses.

Mango Frappé

There are many refreshing iced mango drinks from around the world, from the Indian lassi to the Latin batido to the frappé. Here's my version of this adult mango milkshake.

Serves 2

1 large ripe mango, peeled, cut from the pit, and chopped
1 cup milk
1 tablespoon honey
2 tablespoons Grand Marnier liqueur
1 teaspoon freshly squeezed lime juice
1/4 teaspoon vanilla extract
1 cup vanilla ice cream

Put the mango in a covered container and freeze for at least 1 hour or up to 3 weeks. In a blender, combine the mango, milk, honey, Grand Marnier, lime juice, and vanilla. Purée until smooth. Add the ice cream and blend again until smooth. Serve in chilled glasses.

Lobster and Mango Salad

Two great flavors meet to create a chic new comfort food. Lobster is juicy, flavorful, and abundant in summer, when it is also at its lowest price of the year. Mangos are also at their peak of flavor in summer. The combination of these ingredients makes for a refreshing summertime treat.

Serves 4

2 (2-pound) live Maine lobsters

DRESSING

2 tablespoons Thai fish sauce

1 teaspoon sugar

3 tablespoons freshly squeezed lime juice

3 tablespoons olive oil

1 small Thai chile, seeded and minced

12 large fresh Thai basil leaves, minced

Leaves from 2 sprigs cilantro, minced

1 cup shredded napa cabbage

1 bunch arugula, stems removed

1 small red bell pepper, seeded, deribbed, and thinly sliced

1 large, ripe mango, peeled, cut from the pit, then into julienne

Plunge the lobsters into a large pot of boiling salted water. Cover and boil for 10 minutes. Transfer the lobsters to a bowl and let cool to the touch. Using a clean kitchen towel, tear the claws and legs away from the body. Wrap the towel around the tail and twist, separating it from the body. Place the tail on its side and crush down with the palm of your hand until the shell cracks. Separate the meat from the shell and cut it into 1/2-inch slices. Using a lobster cracker, crack the claws and knuckles of the lobster and remove the flesh with an oyster fork. Use immediately, or cover and refrigerate for up to 24 hours.

To make the dressing: In a small bowl, combine the fish sauce, sugar, lime juice, oil, and chile. Stir in the basil and cilantro.

In a large bowl, toss the cabbage, arugula, bell pepper, and mango with 1/4 cup of the dressing. Arrange the salad on salad plates. Top with overlapping slices of the lobster. Spoon the remaining dressing over the lobster.

Mango Souscaille with Prosciutto

This finger food is derived from an old Martinique recipe. The Creole translation of souscaille *means "under the house" and mango souscaille, "a drunken or marinated mango." Use for a refreshing appetizer or accompaniment for cocktails.*

Serves 4

- 1 large mature green mango, peeled and cut from the pit
- 1/3 cup cold water
- 1 clove garlic, crushed
- 1/4 teaspoon kosher salt
- 1/4 teaspoon freshly ground black pepper
- 1/2 Scotch Bonnet chile, minced, or serrano chile
- Juice of 1 key lime
- 4 slices prosciutto
- 2 sprigs tarragon

Cut the mango into 1/2-inch-thick slices and place them in bowl. In another bowl, mix the water, garlic, salt, pepper, chile, and lime juice together and pour them over the mangos. Cover and refrigerate for at least 30 minutes or, preferably, for 24 hours.

Cut the slices of prosciutto in half lengthwise and place them on a work surface. Place 1 slice of mango and 1 tarragon leaf on each piece and roll up into a cylinder. Serve at once.

Shrimp and Mango Curry

Indian flavors inspired this dish, which combines the sweetness of mango with the complexity of curry powder.

Serves 4

- 2 tablespoons unsalted butter
- 1 onion, diced
- 1 tablespoon minced garlic
- 1 tablespoon minced fresh ginger
- 3 tablespoons Madras curry powder
- 1/2 teaspoon cayenne pepper
- 2 teaspoons plus 1 teaspoon fine sea salt
- 2 cups canned coconut milk
- 2 cups water
- 2 large sweet potatoes, peeled and cut into chunks
- 1/2 teaspoon freshly ground black pepper
- 16 jumbo shrimp, shelled and deveined
- 1 mature green mango, peeled, cut from the pit, and diced
- 3 tablespoons minced green onion, including green parts
- 3 tablespoons chopped fresh cilantro

In a large heavy saucepan, melt the butter over medium heat and sauté the onions and garlic until aromatic, about 3 minutes. Stir in the ginger, curry powder, cayenne, and the 2 teaspoons salt. Stir in coconut milk and water. Bring to a simmer and cook for 5 minutes.

Add the sweet potato and simmer, uncovered, for 15 minutes. Season the shrimp with the 1 teaspoon salt and pepper. Add the shrimp and mango to the pan, return to a simmer and cook for 4 to 5 minutes, or until the shrimp are evenly pink. Serve garnished with green onion and cilantro.

Thai Steak and Mango Salad

Textures play a predominate role in this salad, which combines crisp, crunchy green mango and tender sirloin steak.

Serves 4

- 3 cloves garlic, minced
- 10 sprigs cilantro, stemmed (reserve stems)
- 1 teaspoon kosher salt
- $1/2$ teaspoon freshly ground black pepper
- 3 tablespoons peanut oil
- 12 ounces sirloin steak, trimmed of fat
- Inner leaves from 1 small Bibb lettuce, washed and dried
- 1 small, firm, ripe mango, peeled, cut from the pit, and diced
- 1 cucumber, peeled, seeded, and diced
- 4 large green onions, including light green parts, diced

DRESSING

- 2 tablespoons Thai fish sauce
- 2 tablespoons freshly squeezed lime juice
- 1 tablespoon soy sauce
- 2 teaspoons minced, fresh red Thai or jalapeño chili
- 2 teaspoons packed brown sugar

In a food processor, combine the garlic, cilantro stems, salt, pepper, and 2 tablespoons of the oil. Pulse to make a smooth paste. Spread the paste on both sides of the steak. In a large, heavy skillet, cook the steak 3 to 4 minutes on each side for medium rare. Remove from the pan and let cool.

Cut the steak into thin strips. Divide the lettuce leaves among 4 plates and arrange the mango, cucumber, green onions, and strips of steak on top.

To make the dressing: In a small bowl, combine all the ingredients and stir until the sugar is dissolved.

To serve, drizzle the salad with the dressing and scatter the reserved cilantro leaves over the top.

Spice-Rubbed Jumbo Scallops with Mango and Papaya Salsa

The scallops are dusted with a Southwestern-influenced toasted spice rub. They can be served hot or cold, making this an easy dish for entertaining. Serve on large tropical-colored plates.

Serves 4

SPICE RUB

2 tablespoons cumin seeds

1 tablespoon coriander seeds

1 tablespoon whole black peppercorns

2 star anise pods

1/4 cup hot paprika

1 tablespoon dry mustard

1 tablespoon packed brown sugar

1 1/2 tablespoons kosher salt

---

12 jumbo sea scallops

2 tablespoons olive oil

2 cups Mango and Papaya Salsa (page 112)

Leaves from 4 sprigs cilantro

To make the spice rub: In a small, heavy skillet, toast the cumin, coriander, peppercorns, and star anise pods over medium heat for about 2 minutes or until aromatic. Remove from heat and let cool. In a spice grinder, grind the spices coarsely. Empty into a shallow bowl and stir in the paprika, mustard, sugar, and salt.

Rinse and pat the scallops dry. Roll them in the spice rub to coat completely. Drizzle the coated scallops with olive oil. Heat a large cast-iron skillet over medium-high heat and sear the scallops for 2 minutes on each side, or until well browned.

To serve as an hors d'oeuvre, halve the scallops crosswise into disks and spoon a small amount of salsa onto each scallop half, then garnish with a cilantro leaf. Or, to serve as an appetizer, leave the scallops whole. Spoon some salsa onto each small plate, top with scallops, and garnish with cilantro leaves.

Mango-Shrimp Cocktail

Mango and seafood are fast friends. Here's a twist on that American favorite, the shrimp cocktail. The ingredients in this dish would be as familiar in Brazil as they are in Thailand, both hotbeds of mango passion. I like to serve this in high-stemmed blue Mexican glasses.

Serves 4

2 small ripe mangos, peeled and cut from the pit
1 small red onion, diced
1/2 cup diced cucumber
1/2 cup diced watermelon
1 small jalapeño chile, seeded and diced
2 tablespoons freshly squeezed lime juice
1 tablespoon extra-virgin olive oil
2 tablespoons chopped fresh cilantro
1 teaspoon kosher salt
1/2 teaspoon freshly ground black pepper
12 jumbo shrimp, shelled, deveined, cooked, and chilled
2 tablespoons crushed peanuts

Cut 1 mango into eight 1-inch-wide wedges for garnish. Cut the remaining mango into 1/2-inch dice.

To make the salsa: In a large bowl, combine the diced mango, red onion, cucumber, watermelon, chile, lime juice, olive oil, cilantro, salt, and pepper. Mix well, cover, and refrigerate for at least 30 minutes or up to 4 hours.

Divide the salsa among 4 stemmed glasses. Place 3 shrimp on the rim of each glass.

Garnish each with 2 mango wedges and sprinkle with 1/2 tablespoon peanuts.

Crab and Mango Salad

This salad can be made with either fresh or dried mango slices. Dried mango is simple to prepare at home with a dehydrator or a very low oven: Very thinly slice a mango using a mandoline or a sharp knife. Place the slices in a dehydrator set at 125° for 4 to 5 hours, or in an oven set no higher than 140°, until dry and ridged.

Serves 4

- 3 tablespoons freshly squeezed lime juice
- 2 tablespoons Thai fish sauce
- 2 tablespoons sugar
- 1 small ripe mango, peeled, cut from the pit, and diced
- 2 cups fresh lump crabmeat, picked over for shell
- 2 tablespoons grated fresh coconut or flaked dried coconut
- 1/2 cup coconut milk
- 2 tablespoons chopped green onion, including some green parts
- 1 teaspoon peanut oil
- 1/8 teaspoon red pepper flakes
- 10 fresh cilantro leaves
- 10 fresh basil leaves
- 10 fresh mint leaves
- 1 large ripe mango, peeled, cut from the pit, and cut into 1/4-inch slices

In a small bowl, combine the lime juice, fish sauce, and sugar, stirring to dissolve the sugar. Pour all but 1 teaspoon of the lime mixture into a medium bowl. Reserve the remaining lime mixture for the dressing. Add the diced mango, crabmeat, coconut, coconut milk, and green onion to the medium bowl and mix gently. Cover and refrigerate for 30 minutes.

To make the dressing: In medium bowl, whisk the reserved lime mixture and peanut oil together. Stir in the pepper flakes and herb leaves.

Set a 3-inch ring mold on a plate and place one-eighth of the crab mixture in the mold. Top with a mango slice, then one-eighth of the herb salad. Repeat the layering a second time. Repeat with the remaining plates. If you don't have a ring mold, mound the crabmeat mixture to layer.

To serve, drizzle the salad with the dressing and dot the plate with any remaining salad mixture.

Tuna and Mango Sashimi Salad

An elegant salad with Hawaiian flavors. I suggest using the Carabao mango here, if available, but any fully ripe mango will work well.

Serves 4

16 ounces sashimi-quality tuna steak

2 tablespoons finely chopped green onion, including some green parts

2 tablespoons minced fresh cilantro

3 tablespoons soy sauce

1 tablespoon minced Thai chile

1 teaspoon minced garlic

2 tablespoons minced fresh ginger

2 tablespoons Asian sesame oil

1 large ripe mango, peeled, cut from the pit, and cut into 1-inch cubes

1 tablespoon sesame seeds, toasted (see note)

Cut the tuna into 1-inch cubes and place in a medium bowl. Add the green onion, cilantro, soy sauce, and chile. In a small bowl, combine the garlic and ginger. In a small saucepan, heat the sesame oil until it starts to smoke. Pour into the ginger mixture and mix well. Pour the ginger mixture into the tuna mixture and toss well. Cover and refrigerate for 2 hours.

To serve, carefully fold the mango into the tuna mixture. Serve on salad plates, sprinkled with the sesame seeds.

Toasting Sesame Seeds: In a heavy pan over medium heat, slowly toast the sesame seeds, continuously shaking the pan and watching carefully until the seeds are just golden brown.

Mango-Braised Drumsticks

Turpentine mangos are wonderful-tasting, but also abun-
dant in fiber. They are a good choice for cooking, since the
fiber breaks down during the cooking process. Tommy
Atkins or Haden mangos could be used here, as well. Drum-
sticks, one of those underutilized parts of the chicken, are a
good value for the home cook. This is an easy dish for Sun-
day evening supper. Cardamom pods can be found in
Indian Markets and specialty food stores.

Serves 4

4 tablespoons olive oil
1 onion, thinly sliced
2 teaspoons minced garlic
2 teaspoons minced fresh ginger
1 small jalapeño chili, seeded and diced
Seeds from 3 cardamom pods, crushed
1-inch piece cinnamon stick
10 chicken drumsticks
2 teaspoons kosher salt
1 large ripe mango, peeled, cut from the pit, and diced
1/2 cup dry white wine
3 tablespoons chopped fresh cilantro

In a large skillet over medium heat, heat 3 tablespoons of
the oil and sauté the onion until soft, about 5 minutes. Stir
in the garlic, ginger, jalapeño, cardamom seeds, and cinnamon. Cook, stirring frequently, until the onion is golden
brown, about 5 minutes more. Remove from the pan and
set aside, reserving the pan for the chicken.

Season the drumsticks with the salt. Add the remaining
1 tablespoon oil to the skillet and heat over medium high
heat. Add the chicken and cook on all sides until lightly
browned, about 5 minutes. Add the mango, onion mixture,
and wine. Cover and simmer over low heat for 25 minutes,
or until the chicken is tender. To serve, garnish with fresh
cilantro.

Mango and Avocado Salad

This beautiful composed salad is drizzled with a hot, sweet, and sour Southeast Asian sauce. It makes a refreshing dish for a Sunday brunch.

Serves 4

> 1 large European (hothouse) cucumber, peeled, sliced lengthwise, seeded, and cut into $1/4$ -inch crosswise slices
>
> 1 cup cherry tomatoes, halved
>
> $1/2$ cup cooked green beans, finely sliced
>
> $1/2$ cup bean sprouts
>
> $1/3$ cup rice vinegar
>
> 2 tablespoons freshly squeezed lime juice
>
> 2 red Thai chiles, seeded and minced
>
> 2 teaspoons sugar
>
> 1 small ripe mango peeled, cut from the pit, and sliced
>
> 1 avocado, peeled, pitted, and sliced
>
> $1/4$ cup fresh mint, cut into julienne

In a medium bowl, toss the cucumber, tomatoes, beans, and bean sprouts together. Cover and refrigerate for at least 1 hour, or up to 4 hours. In a small bowl, combine the vinegar, lime juice, chiles, and sugar. Stir until the sugar dissolves.

To serve, arrange the salad mixture, avocado, and mango slices on 4 salad plates. Drizzle with the dressing and garnish with the mint.

MAIN DISHES

Grilled Mahimahi with Mango Sauce and Mango-Shrimp Salsa

(Pictured on preceding page)

This mango sauce is quite versatile. It can be used for poultry, meat, and even shellfish. If you like, double the sauce recipe and store it in the refrigerator for up to 2 weeks.

Serves 4

MANGO SAUCE

2 Roma (plum) tomatoes

1/2 large ripe mango, peeled, cut from the pit, and chopped

1/2 onion, diced

1/2 teaspoon minced garlic

1/2 small jalapeño chile, seeded and diced

21/2 tablespoons cider vinegar

1/4 cup packed dark brown sugar

1 tablespoon dijon mustard

1/2 teaspoon ground cumin

1 teaspoon dried thyme

1 teaspoon dried oregano

2/3 cup freshly squeezed orange juice

2 teaspoons kosher salt

1/2 teaspoon freshly ground black pepper

———

4 (6-ounce) mahimahi fillets

1/2 tablespoon olive oil

1 teaspoon kosher salt

1/2 teaspoon freshly ground black pepper

———

Mango-Shrimp Salsa (recipe follows)

Light a fire in a charcoal grill or heat a grill pan over high heat. Grill the tomatoes on all sides until charred. In a medium saucepan, combine the tomatoes with all the remaining sauce ingredients. Bring to a simmer over low heat and cook for about 15 minutes, or until thickened. Transfer to a blender and purée until smooth.

Coat the mahimahi with the olive oil and season with salt and pepper. Oil the grill grids or pan and grill the mahimahi on the first side for about 3 minutes, or until lightly browned. Turn, baste with the mango sauce, and cook for 2 to 3 minutes, or until opaque throughout. Brush the fillets with the remaining sauce and serve on a bed of Mango-Shrimp Salsa.

Mango-Shrimp Salsa

Makes 4 cups

2 firm, ripe mangos, peeled, cut from the pit, and cut into $1/2$-inch dice

1 small red onion, finely diced

$1/2$ cup $1/4$-inch diced cucumber

$1/2$ cup $1/4$-inch diced watermelon

1 small jalapeno chile, stemmed, seeded, and minced

1 cup cooked rock shrimp

2 tablespoons freshly squeezed lime juice

1 tablespoon extra-virgin olive oil

2 tablespoons minced fresh cilantro

1 teaspoon kosher salt

$1/2$ teaspoon freshly ground black pepper

In a large bowl, combine all the ingredients and mix together well. Cover and refrigerate for at least 30 minutes, or up to 24 hours.

Seared Herb-Coated Tuna with Saffron-Macadamia-Mango Rice

A cilantro, basil, and mint coating adds an aromatic and refreshing note to this dish of seared rare tuna. Amchoor is a powder made from dried green mangos. In Hindi, aam means "mango" and choor means "powder." In this dish, it adds a hint of acidity that balances the richness of the fish. Look for the amchoor in Indian markets.

Serves 4

4 (6-ounce) 1-inch tuna steaks
1 tablespoon Asian sesame oil
3 teaspoon amchoor (green mango powder)
1 teaspoon kosher salt
1 large star anise pod, finely crushed
1/2 teaspoon freshly ground black pepper
2 tablespoons minced fresh cilantro
2 tablespoons minced fresh basil
2 tablespoons minced fresh mint
Hot and Sour Mango Relish (page 108)
Saffron-Macadamia-Mango Rice (recipe follows)

Brush the tuna on all sides with the sesame oil. In a small bowl, combine 1 teaspoon of the amchoor, the salt, star anise, and pepper. Season the tuna with the spice mixture on both sides. In a shallow bowl, combine and mix the cilantro, basil, and mint. Roll the tuna in the herbs to coat evenly.

Heat a large, heavy skillet over high heat until very hot. For rare, sear the tuna for 1 minute on the first side and about 1 minute on the second side. If medium doneness is preferred, sear the tuna for approximately 11/2 minutes on each side. Transfer to a cutting board, and let stand for 2 minutes.

To serve, cut each steak into 1/4-inch-thick slices and fan on a warmed plate. Spoon the mango relish on top. Garnish with the remaining 2 teaspoons amchoor. Serve the rice alongside.

Saffron-Macadamia-Mango Rice

Serves 4 to 6

- **1 pound basmati rice**
- **2 tablespoons clarified butter (see note)**
- **1/2 cup macadamia nuts**
- **2 whole cloves**
- **2 cardamom pods**
- **1-inch piece cinnamon stick**
- **10 whole black peppercorns**
- **1/2 teaspoon saffron, soaked in 1 tablespoon of hot water**
- **1 teaspoon kosher salt**
- **3 cups water**
- **2 tablespoons raisins**
- **1 ripe mango, peeled, cut from the pit and diced**

Rinse rice under cold water and soak for 30 minutes. Drain.

In a large saucepan, heat the butter over medium low heat. Add the macadamia nuts and continuously shake the pan until the nuts turn golden brown. With a slotted spoon, transfer the macadamia nuts to a small bowl. To the same pan and butter, add all of the whole spices and stir constantly for 2 minutes.

Stir the rice into the spice mixture. Add the saffron and salt and stir until the rice is well coated. Add the water and bring to a boil. Decrease heat, cover the pan, and simmer for about 15 minutes, or until the liquid has been absorbed. Remove from the heat and stir in the mango, macadamia nuts, and raisins. Cover and let set for 5 minutes before serving.

Clarifying Butter: Using double the amount of desired clarified butter, melt sweet butter in a small saucepan over medium heat. Remove from heat and let cool slightly. Using a small ladle, skim the white curd off the top and discard. Carefully spoon the clarified butter from the pot, leaving any water and whey at the bottom.

Lamb Chops with Dried Mango and Ginger

This recipe uses green mango in two forms, powdered and fresh, to add exotic flavors and depth of taste to savory lamb chops. Look for the amchoor in Indian markets.

Serves 4

SPICE PASTE
- 3/4 cup molasses
- 3/4 cup water
- 6 tablespoons amchoor (green mango powder)
- 1 teaspoon kosher salt
- 1/2 teaspoon cayenne pepper
- 1/2 teaspoon cumin seeds, toasted (see note)
- 1/2 teaspoon freshly ground black pepper
- 2 tablespoons minced fresh ginger
- 1 tablespoon minced garlic
- 2 tablespoons chopped fresh cilantro

- 8 large lamb loin chops
- 1 teaspoon kosher salt
- 1/2 teaspoon freshly ground black pepper
- 2 tablespoons olive oil
- Green Mango Raita (recipe follows)
- 4 sprigs mint

To make the spice paste: In a small saucepan, combine the molasses, water, and amchoor. Bring to a boil and decrease the heat to a simmer, cook for 5 minutes, and whisk in the salt, cayenne, cumin, and pepper. Simmer for 5 minutes, or until the mixture thickens. Remove from the heat and let cool. In a food processor, combine the molasses mixture, ginger, garlic, and cilantro. Purée until smooth.

Preheat the oven to 350°. Season the lamb with the salt and pepper. In a large cast-iron pan over high heat, heat the olive oil and brown the chops for 1 to 2 minutes on the first side, and 2 minutes on the second side. Remove the pan from heat, brush the chops on both sides with the spice paste, and transfer the pan to the oven. For medium rare, roast for 6 to 8 minutes, basting with the spice paste and turning the meat every 3 minutes.

Serve the chops on a bed of raita and garnish each serving with a mint sprig.

Toasting Cumin Seeds: Heat a small cast-iron pan over medium heat. Add the cumin seeds, shaking the pan vigorously, to brown them well without burning. When the seeds are aromatic, remove them from heat.

Green Mango Raita: Beat 1 cup plain yogurt with a fork until smooth and creamy. Add 1 peeled and diced small green mango, 3 tablespoons sliced green onion, $1/2$ teaspoon toasted and ground cumin, $1/2$ teaspoon minced garlic, a pinch of cayenne, and 1 teaspoon minced orange zest. Cover and refrigerate for at least 1 hour and up to 2 days. Season to taste with salt. Makes 2 cups.

Creole Fried Chicken with Mango

In the Caribbean, cooks would use bitter oranges in this Creole dish, but since they are not readily available here, lime juice is added to regular orange juice for a similar bright acidity.

Serves 4

- 2 large ripe mangos, peeled
- 1 tablespoon minced garlic
- 1/4 cup minced shallots
- 1/2 cup freshly squeezed orange juice
- 1/4 cup freshly squeezed lime juice
- 1/4 cup dark rum
- 2 teaspoons minced Scotch Bonnet chile, or serrano chile
- 1/2 teaspoon ground cumin
- 3 tablespoons packed dark brown sugar
- 2 tablespoons kosher salt
- 3 tablespoons red wine vinegar
- 1 cup canola oil
- 1 (3-pound) chicken, cut into serving pieces
- 1 cup all-purpose flour
- 1 teaspoon freshly ground black pepper
- 1/4 teaspoon cayenne pepper

Carefully cut the cheeks from the mangos and trim the remaining flesh from the pit. Reserve the whole cheeks for sautéing and finely chop the remaining flesh for the marinade.

To make the marinade: In a large bowl, combine the chopped mango, garlic, shallots, orange juice, lime juice, rum, chile, cumin, sugar, 1 tablespoon of the salt, the red wine vinegar, and 1 tablespoon of the oil. Add the chicken and turn to coat. Cover and refrigerate for at least 2 hours, and up to 24 hours.

In a shallow bowl, combine the flour, remaining 1 tablespoon salt, pepper, and cayenne. Stir to mix well. Dredge the chicken in the seasoned flour. In a large, heavy pan over medium-high heat, heat the remaining oil until very hot and fry the chicken in batches, browning each side for 5 to 6 minutes. Using tongs, transfer to paper towels to drain.

In the same oil, over medium heat, sauté the mango cheeks on each side for 2 to 3 minutes, or until well browned. Serve the chicken on warmed plates, with a mango piece alongside.

Panfried Soft-Shell Crabs
with Green Mango Slaw

Soft-shell crabs are blue crabs in their molting stage, when the crab sheds its outer shell in order to grow. The beauty of soft-shell crabs is that you can eat them whole, shell and all. Their sweet flavor is enhanced by panfrying.

Serves 4

- **8 large soft-shell crabs**
- **2 cups cornmeal**
- **1 cup all-purpose flour**
- **1 tablespoon kosher salt**
- **1 teaspoon ground fennel**
- **1 teaspoon freshly ground black pepper**
- **2 cups buttermilk**
- **2 tablespoons clarified butter (see page 91)**
- **$^1/_4$ cup olive oil**
- **3 cups Green Mango Slaw (page 111)**
- **2 limes, quartered**

With scissors, cut off the face of each crab just below the eyes. Turn the crab over and lift up and remove its triangular tail. Lift the flaps on each side of the crab and remove the fatty gills with your fingers. In a medium bowl, combine the cornmeal and flour. Add the salt, fennel, and pepper, mixing well. Pour the buttermilk into another medium bowl. Add the crabs to the buttermilk and toss gently. Drain. Gently turn the crabs in the cornmeal mixture to coat them completely.

In a large skillet, melt the butter with the oil over medium-high heat. Add 2 or 3 crabs (do not overcrowd the pan). Cook for 3 to 4 minutes per side, until golden brown and crispy. Transfer to paper towels to drain. Keep warm in a low oven while you cook the remaining crabs.

To serve, mound the mango slaw in the center of each plate and top with 2 soft-shell crabs. Garnish each plate with 2 lime wedges.

Ale-Roasted Pompano
with Mango-Cashew Salsa

The firm, green Rosa mango from Brazil, with its lush tropical aroma, really complements cashew nuts, but any crisp green mango could be used here. If pompano is not available, whole black bass, snapper, or striped bass could be substituted.

Serves 4

2 (1^1/$_2$–1^3/$_4$ pounds) whole pompano
1 cup ale
^{1}/$_2$ cup diced celery
4 sprigs thyme
1 teaspoon allspice berries
1 teaspoon kosher salt
^{1}/$_2$ teaspoon freshly ground black pepper
1^1/$_2$ tablespoons olive oil

CASHEW SALSA
^{1}/$_2$ cup unsalted cashews
^{1}/$_2$ cup diced seeded tomatoes
^{1}/$_2$ cup diced ripe mango
3 tablespoons finely chopped green onion, including some green parts
3 tablespoons diced seeded jalapeño chiles
1 teaspoon freshly squeezed lime juice
2 tablespoons fresh cilantro leaves
1^1/$_2$ teaspoons olive oil
2 teaspoons kosher salt
1 teaspoon freshly ground black pepper

With a sharp knife, score the fish by cutting 3 shallow crosswise slits in the flesh. Place the pompano in a roasting pan. In a small bowl, combine the ale, celery, thyme, allspice, salt, and pepper. Whisk the olive oil into the ale mixture and pour over the pompano.

To make the salsa: In a small bowl, combine all the ingredients. Stir until evenly coated with the lime juice and olive oil.

Preheat the oven to 375°. Bake the fish for 5 minutes. Baste the fish with the pan juices and continue to roast for another 5 to 7 minutes, or until the skin near the exposed flesh is golden brown. Remove from the oven.

The pompano may be served whole or in fillets. If fillets are preferred, remove the head and tail of one fish. Cut to the bone at each of the 3 slits on one side of one fish. For 2 center cut chunks, slide a knife from the center cut to the left cut, pulling the flesh off the bone and again, from the center cut to the right cut. For the 2 smaller outside chunks, remove the flesh in the same manner. Repeat for opposite side of the fish. Repeat for the remaining fish.

To serve, drizzle with the juices from the roasting pan, and garnish with the salsa.

Roast Pork Loin with Mango Mojo and Yellow Plantains

In this Cuban-inspired dish, marinating the pork in the mango mojo allows the mango flavor to perfume the meat. Use plantains with a yellow skin; they are underripe and will stay firm when cooked.

Serves 4

> 2 pounds pork tenderloin, trimmed of excess fat
> 2 cups Mango Mojo (page 109)
> 2 tablespoons olive oil
> 1 tablespoon kosher salt
> 1/2 tablespoon freshly ground black pepper
> 4 yellow plantains, peeled, and cut into 2-inch pieces on the diagonal

Put the pork in a baking dish just large enough to hold it. Pour in the mango mojo, cover, and refrigerate for at least 2 hours or up to 24 hours.

Preheat the oven to 400°. Remove the pork from the marinade and pat dry. Set the marinade aside. Brush the pork with olive oil and season with salt and pepper. Put the pork in a roasting pan and roast for 10 minutes, then decrease the temperature to 350°. Turn the meat over and pour half of the reserved marinade over the pork. Add the plantains and roast for another 35 to 40 minutes, or until the pork is cooked through and the plantains are golden brown. Let the meat rest for 5 minutes.

To serve, slice the meat across the grain and fan the slices on a large serving platter. Arrange the plantains on the sides of the platter. Spoon any pan juices over the pork.

Chicken and Green Mango Stew

The Kyo Savoy and Nom Doc Mai are two excellent green mango varieties that can be used in this Southeast-Asian inspired dish. Any crisp green mango may also be used.

Serves 6

1 (3-pound) whole chicken, rinsed
2 cups chopped onion
1 cup chopped leeks (white part only)
1 cup chopped celery
1 large jalapeño chile, seeded and minced
8 large cloves garlic, minced
4 teaspoons kosher salt
2 cups canned coconut milk
2 cups 1-inch cubed peeled mature green mango
1 cup 1-inch cubed peeled yuca
1 cup 1-inch cubed peeled sweet potato
1 cup 1-inch cubed peeled potato
2 cups 1-inch cubed peeled calabaza or acorn squash
1 cup 1-inch cubed peeled green plantain
6 tablespoons freshly squeezed lime juice
1 tablespoon freshly ground black pepper
1/2 cup chopped fresh cilantro

Put the chicken in a pot just large enough to hold it comfortably. Add cold water to cover and bring to a boil. Decrease heat to a simmer and cook, uncovered, for 5 minutes. Skim off any foam that rises to the surface. Add the onion, leeks, celery, chile, garlic, and 3 teaspoons of the salt. Bring to a boil, then again decrease heat to a simmer. Cook for 40 minutes, or until tender.

Remove the chicken, set aside and let cool to the touch. Remove the skin and discard. Remove the meat from the carcass and tear into large pieces. Cover and set aside.

Return the chicken bones to the broth and simmer for 30 minutes more. Strain and degrease the broth and set it aside.

Return 2 cups of the broth to the pot. Stir in the coconut milk, the mango and the vegetables, and bring to a boil. Decrease the heat and simmer for 10 minutes, or until the mango and vegetables are just tender.

Return the chicken pieces to the pot and simmer for 5 minutes. Season with the lime juice, pepper, and remaining 1 teaspoon salt. Serve in deep bowls, garnished with cilantro.

Pan-Roasted Lobster with Spicy Mango Glaze

This is a simple dish with a powerful flavor. The glaze calls for a very ripe mango.

Serves 4

SPICY MANGO GLAZE
- 1 teaspoon olive oil
- 1/2 cup red wine vinegar
- 3 tablespoons packed brown sugar
- 2 teaspoons minced jalapeño chile
- 1 teaspoon minced fresh ginger
- 1 very ripe mango, peeled, cut from the pit, and puréed
- Salt and freshly ground black pepper to taste

- 4 (6-ounce) lobster tails, split lengthwise
- 1 teaspoon kosher salt
- 1/4 teaspoon freshly ground black pepper
- 2 teaspoons olive oil
- 1 teaspoon unsalted butter

Preheat the oven to 350°.

To make the glaze: In a small saucepan, heat the oil over medium-high heat and add the vinegar, sugar, chile, and ginger. Bring to a boil, decrease the heat, and simmer for 3 minutes, or until the mixture begins to brown. Stir in the mango. Season with salt and pepper, simmer for 1 minute, and remove from the heat.

Season the lobster tails with the salt and pepper. In a large heavy skillet, over medium-high heat, heat the oil until almost smoking. Add the butter and cook the lobster tails, flesh-side down, for 2 to 3 minutes, or until the flesh begins to turn white and the edges of the shell turn rosy pink. Turn and brush the mango glaze on the lobster meat. Roast in the oven for 8 minutes, until the flesh is opaque throughout.

CONDIMENTS

Preceding page, clockwise from top right: Mango Ketchup, Quick Ripe-Mango Chutney, Green Mango Pickle (Achar), Mango Chow, Mango Jam, and Mango Souscaille (see Mango Souscaille with Prosciutto, page 73)

Hot and Sour Mango Relish

This Vietnamese-inspired relish can be served with fish, shellfish, or poultry. The Vietnamese use Kyo Savoy, a very green, almost blue-skinned mango, but any green mango will do.

Makes 2 cups

> 2 small mature green mangos, peeled and cut from the pit
> 2 tablespoons peanut oil
> 4 ounces dried shrimp
> 2 small serrano chiles, seeded and minced
> 3 small shallots, minced
> 2 tablespoons freshly squeezed lemon juice
> 2 tablespoons Thai fish sauce
> 1 teaspoon sugar
> 1 large green onion, finely chopped, including light green parts

Cut the mango into matchsticks and set aside.

In a small skillet over medium heat, heat the oil and sauté the shrimp until lightly browned. With a slotted spoon, transfer the shrimp to a small bowl. Add all the remaining ingredients including the mango. Toss until all the ingredients are well coated. Place the relish in a hot, sterilized jar and seal with an airtight cover. Refrigerate until ready to use. The relish can keep well for up to 2 weeks.

Raw-Mango Chutney

Green Cambodiana mangos would be ideal in this chutney. Their flesh is deep yellow in color, very juicy, and free from fiber, making it an excellent mango for eating raw. But any green mango could be used here. This chutney is wonderful with fish and seafood. Kaffir lime can be found at Asian markets and specialty food stores.

Makes 4 cups

- 1 teaspoon sesame seeds
- 1 tablespoon red pepper flakes
- 3 mature green mangos, peeled, and cut from the pit, and chopped
- 1 teaspoon kosher salt
- 4 shallots, chopped
- 2 tablespoons grated dried coconut
- 2 leaves kaffir lime, chopped
- 1 tablespoon chopped fresh cilantro
- 2 tablespoons olive oil
- 1 tablespoon black mustard seeds

In a small, dry skillet, toast the sesame seeds and pepper flakes over medium-high heat until fragrant. In a food processor, combine the mangos, sesame seed mixture, salt, shallots, coconut, kaffir leaves, and cilantro and process until coarsely ground.

In a small skillet over medium heat, heat the oil. Add the mustard seeds and cook, shaking the pan, until they start to pop. Pour the mixture into the chutney and mix well.

Pour the chutney into a hot, sterilized jar and seal with an airtight cover. Refrigerate for at least 24 hours before using. The chutney will keep, refrigerated, for 2 to 3 days.

Mango Vinaigrette

Mango vinaigrette is refreshing for a summer salad. I usually mix arugula with Lola Rossa and Bibb lettuce. Try adding some toasted pine nuts, diced mango, and a few grilled shrimp or scallops, or sliced grilled chicken breast.

Makes 3 cups

1 medium ripe mango, peeled and cut from the pit
2 tablespoons minced fresh ginger
2 tablespoons freshly squeezed lime juice
1/4 cup rice vinegar
1 small red bell pepper, seeded, deribbed, and diced
1 small red Thai chile, seeded and minced
1/4 cup minced fresh cilantro
1/4 cup canola oil
2 teaspoons kosher salt
1 teaspoon freshly ground black pepper

Cut one half of the mango into 1/4-inch dice. Chop the other half and remaining flesh coarsely. In a food processor, combine the chopped mango, ginger, lime juice, and rice vinegar. Process until smooth.

In a large bowl, combine the mango purée, bell pepper, chile, and cilantro. Gradually whisk in the oil to make an emulsified sauce. Stir in the salt, pepper, and diced mango. The vinaigrette will keep, covered and refrigerated, for 2 to 3 days.

Mango Mojo

A mojo (pronounced mo-ho) is a pungent Cuban marinating sauce. I suggest marinating in a mojo for at least 30 minutes to allow the flavors to penetrate. The natural sweetness of ripe mango will glaze and brown what ever you roast. This mojo is especially good for pork and shrimp, but also great for all meats, chicken, fish, and shellfish.

Makes 4 cups

- 3 tablespoons olive oil
- 1 large onion, cut into $1/4$-inch dice
- 2 cloves garlic, minced
- 1 tablespoon ground cumin
- 1 teaspoon dried oregano
- 1 tablespoon kosher salt
- 1 teaspoon freshly ground black pepper
- 2 cups freshly squeezed orange juice
- 1 cup dry white wine
- $1/4$ cup freshly squeezed lime juice
- 1 large ripe mango, peeled, cut from the pit, and cut into $1/4$-inch dice

In a medium saucepan over medium heat, heat the olive oil and cook the onion for about 5 minutes, or until soft. Add the garlic and sauté for 1 minute. Add the cumin, oregano, salt, and pepper, and sauté for 2 minutes more. Add the orange juice, white wine, lime juice and the mango. Bring the mixture to a simmer and cook for 15 minutes. Cool for 10 minutes then transfer to a blender and purée until smooth. The mojo may be used immediately. To store, pour into hot, sterilized jars and seal each jar with an airtight cover. The mojo will keep, refrigerated, for 2 to 3 weeks.

Green Mango Pickle (Achar)

Achar is a unique Indian condiment that takes almost two weeks to make, but is worth the time. Serve it with roasted meats, such as leg of lamb. Look for fenugreek and asafoetida in spice stores or Indian markets.

Makes 6 cups

2 pounds unpeeled immature green mangos, cut from the pit and cut into 1-inch cubes

3 tablespoons kosher salt

1/4 cup cumin seeds, coarsely ground

1/4 cup fenugreek seeds, coarsely ground

1/4 cup sesame seeds

1 tablespoon ground turmeric

3 tablespoons cayenne pepper

1 teaspoon ground asafoetida

1 tablespoon minced garlic

1 cup corn oil

2 tablespoons mustard seed

In a medium bowl, combine the mangos and salt. Stir to mix. Cover and let sit overnight. Drain.

In a large bowl, combine the cumin and fenugreek seeds, sesame seeds, turmeric, cayenne, asafoetida, and garlic. In a small saucepan over medium heat, heat the oil until almost smoking. Add the mustard seeds and cook, shaking the pan, until they start to pop. Remove from the heat and let cool completely. Add half of the mustard oil to the spice mixture and mix well.

Add the salted mango to the spice mixture, stirring to coat thoroughly. Pour in the remaining mustard oil and mix well. Transfer to hot, sterilized jars, making sure the oil covers the mango completely. Cover each with a piece of cheesecloth and tie with a piece of string.

Let the jars sit in a warm and sunny place for 4 days. Remove the cheesecloth and cover each jar with an airtight lid. Store in a cool, dark place for at least 1 week before using. The pickle will keep, refrigerated, for 3 to 4 months.

Green Mango Slaw

This "fusion" slaw blends the flavors of Indonesia and the Caribbean. It's a great accompaniment to barbecued ribs.

Makes 4 cups

- 2 large mature green mangos, peeled, cut from the pit, and shredded
- 1 large carrot, peeled and shredded
- 1 small red onion, thinly sliced
- 2 tablespoons chopped fresh mint
- 2 tablespoons chopped fresh basil
- 3 tablespoons chopped fresh cilantro
- 1 teaspoon minced garlic
- 1/4 cup freshly squeezed lime juice
- 2 tablespoons sugar
- 1 teaspoon seeded and minced serrano chile
- 2 tablespoons Thai fish sauce

In a large bowl, combine the mangos, carrot, and onion. Add the mint, basil, and cilantro and toss together. In a small bowl, combine the garlic, lime juice, sugar, chile and fish sauce. Stir until the sugar is dissolved. Pour the lime mixture into the slaw and toss together, coating all the ingredients well. Cover and refrigerate for at least 1 hour, or up to 24 hours before serving.

Mango and Papaya Salsa

Mango salsa is one of the standards of "palm-tree" cuisine. You'll find it served with crab cakes, pan-roasted scallops, fried calamari, grilled grouper, rare tuna, and lobster salad. Here's a version that combines mangos with papaya, another wonderful tropical fruit.

Serves 6

2 large ripe mangos, peeled and cut from the pit

1 large ripe papaya, peeled and seeded

1 red bell pepper, seeded, deribbed, and finely diced

1 red onion, finely diced

1 jalapeño chile, seeded and minced

2 tablespoons minced fresh cilantro

2 teaspoons ground cumin

1 teaspoon kosher salt

3 tablespoons olive oil

Juice of 1 lime

Cut the mangos and papaya into ¼-inch dice. In a large bowl, combine the mangos, papaya, bell pepper, onion, chile, and cilantro. Add the cumin, salt, olive oil, and lime juice and stir to blend. Cover and refrigerate for at least 1 hour, or up to 2 days.

Dried-Fruit Chutney

This chutney has an intense fruit flavor because it is made with dried fruit. Using fresh mangos, green mango powder, and dried mango gives this a three-dimensional flavor. Serve with curry dishes.

Makes 3 cups

> 1 onion, chopped
> 1 large mature green mango, peeled, cut from the pit, and chopped
> 5 cloves garlic
> 1-inch piece fresh ginger, peeled, and coarsely chopped
> 1 teaspoon cumin seeds
> 1/4 cup canola oil
> 1/4 teaspoon ground turmeric
> 1 teaspoon red pepper flakes
> 1 teaspoon amchoor (green mango powder)
> 2 teaspoons kosher salt
> 2 teaspoons packed brown sugar
> 1 cup water
> 1/2 cup diced pitted dates
> 1/2 cup diced dried mango
> 1/4 cup unsalted cashews, coarsely chopped
> 1/4 cup raisins
> 2 tablespoons minced fresh cilantro

In a food processor, combine the onion, mango, garlic, ginger, and cumin. Purée until smooth.

In a medium, heavy saucepan over medium heat, heat the oil and add the turmeric, pepper flakes, amchoor, and salt. Cook, stirring, for 1 minute. Add the mango purée and cook, stirring frequently, until the mixture comes to a boil. Stir in the sugar, water, dates, dried mango, cashews, and raisins. Return to a simmer and cook, uncovered, for about 20 minutes, or until the nuts are softened. Remove from heat and stir in the cilantro. Serve hot or chilled. To store, pour into a hot, sterilized jar and seal with an airtight cover. The chutney will keep, refrigerated, for up to 2 to 3 weeks.

Mango Chow

The ingredients of this simple salsa vary in Latin and Caribbean countries where it's referred to as "chow". In Mexico, it's made without shallots and sold in the markets in small plastic bags. In Trinidad, "chow" includes cilantro and is eaten as a summertime snack. In Jamaica, the fiery Scotch Bonnet chile is substituted for the mild jalapeño.

Makes 2 cups

> 1 firm, ripe mango, peeled, cut from the pit, and cut into 1/4 -inch dice
> 1 large shallot, minced
> 1 large jalapeño chile, stemmed, seeded and cut into coins
> 2 tablespoons freshly squeezed lime juice
> 2 tablespoons chopped fresh cilantro
> 1 teaspoon kosher salt
> 1/2 teaspoon freshly ground black pepper

In a medium bowl, combine the mango, shallot, chile, lime juice, and cilantro. Season with the salt and pepper. The chow will keep, refrigerated, for 1 to 2 days.

Mango Jam

There must be dozens of mango jam recipes in South Florida. This simple one brings out the natural goodness of the mango. I like to use the Ataulfo mango because of its pleasant balance of acidity and sweetness, but any ripe mango can be used.

Makes 8 cups

- **6 pounds ripe mangos, peeled, cut from the pit, and chopped**
- **4 cups water**
- **1 vanilla bean, split lengthwise**
- **6 cups sugar**
- **1/2 teaspoon ground cloves**
- **1/2 teaspoon ground allspice**
- **1 teaspoon minced orange zest**

In a large pot, combine the mangos, water, and vanilla bean. Bring to a boil and cook for 10 to 12 minutes, or until soft enough to mash. Remove the vanilla bean. Press the mango mixture through a medium-mesh sieve or food mill and return to the pot. Add the sugar, cloves, allspice, and orange zest. Gently bring to a boil, stirring frequently to prevent burning, and simmer gently for about 45 minutes, or until thickened. Pour into hot, sterilized jars and seal each jar with an airtight cover. Store in the refrigerator for 2 to 3 months.

Mango-Peach Marmalade

Summertime in a bottle. This marmalade blends the lush flesh of sweet peaches and mangos. The synergy of flavors far exceeds the individual parts.

Makes 8 cups

1 pound firm ripe peaches

3 pounds firm ripe mangos, peeled, cut from the pit, and cut into 2-inch long by $1/2$-inch thick slices

4 cups sugar

1 lemon, cut into thin slices crosswise, and seeded

1 large vanilla bean, split lengthwise

3 tablespoons Cognac

Peel the peaches: Blanch them in boiling water for 1 minute, then plunge them into ice water. Drain, peel, cut in half, and remove the pits. Cut the flesh into thick slices. In a large, stainless-steel saucepan, combine the peaches, mangos, sugar, lemon slices, and vanilla bean. Cover and let stand for 2 hours.

Bring the mixture to a gentle boil, then decrease the heat to a simmer and cook for 20 minutes, or until the fruit is soft. Return to a boil and cook, stirring frequently, for 25 to 30 minutes, or until thickened.

Remove from heat and stir in the Cognac. Remove the vanilla bean, scraping out the seeds into the mixture. Ladle the preserves into hot, sterilized jars and seal each jar with an airtight cover. Store in the refrigerator for 2 to 3 months.

Mango Ketchup

Mango ketchup is very versatile. It can be served with grilled fish, turkey meat loaf, baked potatoes, and fries. It's also good as a simple glaze for grilled or broiled chicken breast and jumbo shrimp. This is a home version of my Chef Allen's mango ketchup which is sold nationwide in gourmet and specialty foods shops.

Makes 4 cups

> 5 ripe mangos, peeled, cut from the pit, and chopped
> 1/4 cup cider vinegar
> 1 tablespoon chopped fresh ginger
> 1 tablespoon chopped fresh garlic
> 1 tablespoon kosher salt
> 1/2 cup sugar
> 1/2 teaspoon ground allspice
> 1/2 teaspoon cayenne pepper
> 1/8 teaspoon ground cloves
> 1/8 teaspoon ground cinnamon

In a food processor, purée the mangos until smooth. Add all the remaining ingredients and pulse together to blend.

In a large, heavy saucepan, simmer the mixture gently, stirring frequently, for about 1 hour, or until quite thick. Pour into hot, sterilized jars and seal each jar with an airtight cover. Store in the refrigerator for up to 4 months.

DESSERTS

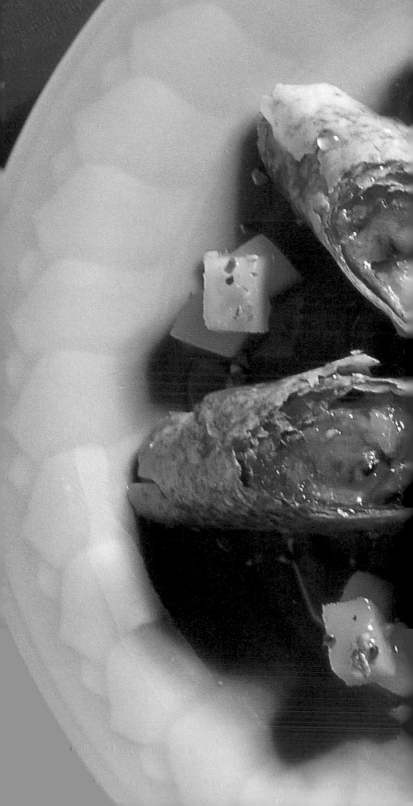

Mango, Banana, and Pistachio Strudel

(Pictured on preceding page)

A complex-flavored mango, such as the Indian Alphonse or Mexican Manila, is perfect for this strudel, but any ripe mango may be used. The touch of cocoa adds an interesting flavor note to the tropical blend of ingredients.

Serves 6

> 1 large ripe mango, peeled, cut from the pit, and diced
> 2 large ripe bananas, peeled and sliced
> 1/2 cup shelled, unsalted pistachios, chopped
> 1 teaspoon vanilla extract
> 2 tablespoons honey
> 1 tablespoon ground cinnamon
> 1 tablespoon unsweetened cocoa powder
> 3 tablespoons sugar
> 6 sheets frozen phyllo, thawed
> 1/4 cup clarified butter, melted (see page 91)

In a large bowl, combine the mango, bananas, pistachios, vanilla, and honey. Mix carefully so as not to crush the pieces of fruit.

In a small bowl, combine the cinnamon, cocoa, and sugar. Remove and reserve 2 tablespoons of the mixture. Place the remaining mixture in a sugar shaker.

Preheat the oven to 350°. Lay 1 sheet of phyllo out on a dry work surface; keep the remaining sheets covered with plastic. Brush the phyllo with butter, then sprinkle with some of the cinnamon mixture. Place another sheet of phyllo on top of the first. Again, brush with butter and sprinkle with the cinnamon mixture. Repeat to make a third layer. Mix 1 tablespoon of the reserved cinnamon mixture into the mango mixture. Place half of the mango mixture along the bottom edge of the layered phyllo sheets and roll up the dough into a cylinder. Brush the outside of the roll with butter and place seam-side down on a baking sheet. Repeat to make a second strudel. Sprinkle both with the remaining cinnamon mixture from the shaker.

Bake the strudels for 15 minutes, or until golden brown. Remove from the oven and let cool slightly before cutting and serving warm.

Mango Sour Cream Crumb Cake

This is wonderful served with freshly brewed Darjeeling tea.

Serves 8 to 10

> **4 large egg yolks**
> **1 cup sour cream**
> **1 1/2 teaspoons vanilla extract**
> **2 cups sifted cake flour**
> **1 cup sugar**
> **1/2 teaspoon baking powder**
> **1/2 teaspoon baking soda**
> **1/4 teaspoon fine salt**
> **3/4 cup (1 1/2 sticks) unsalted butter, at room temperature**

STREUSEL TOPPING
> **1/3 cup sugar**
> **1 cup pecans**
> **1 1/2 teaspoons ground cinnamon**
> **1/2 cup unsifted cake flour**
> **4 tablespoons cold unsalted butter**
> **1/2 teaspoon vanilla extract**
> **3 large ripe mangos, peeled, cut from the pit, and sliced**

Preheat the oven to 350°. In a medium bowl, combine the egg yolks, 1 tablespoon of the sour cream, and the vanilla. In a large bowl, blend together the cake flour, sugar, baking powder, baking soda, and salt. Add the butter and the remaining sour cream. Mix on low speed until the dry ingredients are moistened. Increase to medium speed and gradually beat in the egg mixture until blended.

To make the topping: In a food processor, combine the sugar, pecans, and cinnamon. Pulse until the nuts are coarsely chopped. Remove 3/4 cup of this mixture and reserve. To the mixture remaining in the machine, add the cake flour, butter, and vanilla. Pulse briefly to form a coarse, crumbly mixture.

Pour the cake batter into a buttered, 10-inch springform pan. Sprinkle with the reserved nut mixture and top evenly with the mango slices. Scatter with the streusel topping. Bake for 55 minutes, or until the cake is golden brown and a tester inserted in the center comes out clean.

Let cool in the pan on a wire rack for 10 minutes. Remove the sides of the pan and let cool completely before serving.

Ginger-Rum Grilled Pineapple with Mango Sorbet

A refreshing dessert for a backyard barbecue. When the chicken and ribs and burgers come off the grill, add the marinated pineapple.

Serves 4

- **4 tablespoons unsalted butter, melted**
- **$1/2$ cup sugar**
- **1 teaspoon grated lime zest**
- **2 tablespoons freshly squeezed lime juice**
- **1 tablespoon grated fresh ginger**
- **$1/2$ teaspoon ground cinnamon**
- **$1/8$ teaspoon ground allspice**
- **1 large ripe pineapple, peeled, cored, and cut into $3/4$-inch-thick crosswise slices**
- **$1/2$ cup dark rum**
- **1 pint Mango Sorbet (recipe follows)**
- **$1/2$ cup macadamia nuts, toasted (see note)**

Light a fire in a charcoal grill or preheat a gas grill to medium-high.

In a large baking dish, combine the butter, sugar, lime zest and juice, ginger, cinnamon, and allspice. Add the pineapple, toss the coat, and let sit for 15 minutes.

Grill the pineapple slices for 5 minutes on each side, or until lightly browned. Transfer to dessert dishes. Pour the rum over the hot pineapple. Using a long-handled match, very carefully ignite and let the rum burn off.

To serve, place a scoop of sorbet in the center of each pineapple slice and top with toasted macadamia nuts.

Toasting Macadamia Nuts: Warm a small skillet over medium-high heat. Add the macadamia nuts. Continuously shake the pan to prevent the nuts from browning too much on any one side. When golden brown, remove from heat and let cool.

Mango Sorbet

The Indian Alphonse or Dasheri are both great in desserts. Their complex flavors shine in this simple sorbet.

Makes 2 pints

  2 large, ripe mangos, peeled and cut from the pit
  1 cup sugar
  1 cup water
  1 teaspoon lime

Purée the mango pieces in a food processor. Push the purée through a fine sieve, to remove any fibers. Set aside.

In a small saucepan over medium heat, combine the sugar, water and lime juice. Simmer, stirring constantly, for 5 minutes. Remove from the heat and let cool.

Combine the syrup with the mango purée in a large mixing bowl. Pour the mixture into an ice cream machine and freeze according to manufacturer's instructions.

Country Mango Tarts

These rustic tarts are made without a tart pan by folding the edges of the pastry over the mango slices. Enjoy!

Makes 6

PASTRY DOUGH
- 1 1/4 cups unbleached all-purpose flour
- 2 tablespoons sugar
- 1/4 teaspoon fine sea salt
- 1/2 cup (1 stick) cold unsalted butter, cut into 1 /2-inch dice
- 4 ounces cold cream cheese, cut into 1/2-inch dice
- 2 teaspoons freshly squeezed lime juice
- 1 tablespoon ice water

- 6 tablespoons sugar
- 2 large ripe mangos, peeled, and cut from the pit
- 2 tablespoons freshly squeezed lime juice
- 1 teaspoon minced fresh ginger
- 2 tablespoons milk

To make the dough: In the bowl of an electric mixer fitted with a paddle, combine the flour, sugar, and salt. Mix on low speed until blended. Add the butter and cream cheese and mix on medium speed to a pebbly consistency. Add the lime juice and water; continue to mix just until the dough forms into a ball. Transfer to a lightly floured surface. Cut into 6 equal pieces and shape each into a disk. Transfer to a plate, cover with plastic wrap, and refrigerate for 30 minutes, or until firm.

Preheat the oven to 400°. Remove the dough from the refrigerator and let stand for 5 minutes. Roll each disk into a 6-inch-diameter round and place the rounds on a parchment paper-lined baking sheet. Brush the pastry dough with milk and sprinkle with 2 tablespoons of the sugar.

Cut the mangos into 1/4-inch lengthwise slices. In a medium bowl, carefully mix together the mangos, lime juice, the remaining 4 tablespoons of sugar, and the ginger. Arrange the mango slices on each pastry round, leaving a 1-inch border. Fold the edges of the pastry over, pleating as you go.

Bake for 15 minutes, or until the edges of the pastry and the mangos are both golden brown.

Mango and Almond Macaroon Tart

Mangos take on new characteristics when they are caramelized. Here, they are paired with nuts, a natural combination. The macaroon topping adds a chewy counterpoint.

Serves 8

- 1/4 cup packed light brown sugar
- 1 teaspoon minced fresh ginger
- 2 tablespoons freshly squeezed lime juice
- 3 large ripe mangos, peeled, cut from the pit, and cut into 1/4 -inch-thick slices

MACAROON TOPPING

- 1 cup blanched almonds, finely ground
- 1 cup sugar
- 1/2 teaspoon vanilla extract
- 1/2 teaspoon grated lemon zest
- 2 large egg whites

Preheat the oven to 350°. In a 10-inch round cake pan, combine the brown sugar, ginger, and lime juice. On top of the stove, place over low heat until the sugar is dissolved. Remove from the heat and place the mango slices in the pan in one layer, to form a pinwheel shape. Return the pan to low heat for 5 minutes to lightly caramelize the mango, taking care not to burn the sugar.

In a medium bowl, combine the almonds, sugar, vanilla, and lemon zest. Whisk the egg whites until foamy and stir into the almond mixture. Press this topping gently onto the top of the mango layer.

Bake in the lower third of the oven for 35 minutes, or until the tart edges are golden brown. Remove from the oven and let cool on a wire rack for 20 minutes. Invert onto a large plate to unmold. Let cool completely before serving.

Mango Cobbler

Here's an exotic, tropical version of the cobblers of my youth. Both Irwin and Edward mangos are good choices for this cobbler, but any ripe mangos can be used. Serve with a scoop of vanilla ice cream.

Serves 6

- 4 large ripe mangos, peeled, cut from the pit, and sliced
- 1 teaspoon ground ginger
- 1 teaspoon ground cinnamon
- $1/2$ cup freshly squeezed orange juice

TOPPING

- 1 cup unbleached all-purpose flour
- 1 tablespoon sugar
- $1/4$ teaspoon fine sea salt
- $1 1/2$ teaspoons baking powder
- 3 tablespoons unsalted butter, at room temperature
- $1/2$ cup milk
- $1/4$ cup confectioners' sugar

Preheat the oven to 350°. In a 9-inch baking dish, combine the mangos, ginger, cinnamon, and orange juice. Toss together to coat.

To make the topping: In a small bowl, combine the flour, sugar, salt, and baking powder. Stir to blend. Add the butter and mix until incorporated to a sandy consistency. Stir in the milk just until smooth. Dollop this topping onto the mango mixture, spreading to cover most of the top.

Bake for 25 minutes, or until golden brown. Dust with confectioners' sugar and serve warm.

Indian Mango Ice Cream

Indian-style ice cream, called kulfi, is a creamy, rich, still-frozen dessert that is traditionally served in small, conical-shaped aluminum molds. You can use ramekins or custard dishes instead.

Serves 4

> **6 cups milk**
> **2/3 cup sugar**
> **11/2 large, ripe mangos, peeled, cut from the pit, and sliced**
> **1/4 cup pistachio nuts, coarsely chopped**

In a medium, heavy saucepan, bring the milk to a boil over high heat. Decrease the heat to very low and simmer until the milk is reduced to 11/2 cups, stirring constantly for the first 15 minutes and then at 2 to 3 minute intervals. Take care that the milk does not scorch on the bottom or boil over; adjust the heat accordingly. Add the sugar and stir until dissolved. Remove the pan from heat and let cool completely.

In a blender, purée one third of the mango until smooth. Measure 1/2 cup of the mango purée and add to the milk mixture. Mix well, and stir in the pistachio nuts. Pour into six 4-ounce ramekins or custard dishes and freeze for about 5 hours, or until firm.

A few minutes before serving, remove the molds from the freezer. Dip the bottom of each into a bowl of hot water for a few seconds and invert and unmold onto a dessert plate. Serve garnished with the remaining mango slices.

Mangos with Sticky Rice

This Southeast Asian dish is finished with coconut rum, fusing it with the flavors of the Caribbean. Sticky rice, also called sweet or glutinous rice, is available in Asian markets.

Serves 6

- **1 1/2 cups sticky rice**
- **1 cup canned coconut milk**
- **2 tablespoons sugar**
- **1/2 teaspoon fine seasalt**
- **3 large, ripe mangos, peeled and cut from the pit**
- **2 tablespoons coconut rum**

Place the rice in a sieve and rinse under cold water until the water runs clear. Place the rice in a bowl, cover with water and let soak for at least 4 hours and up to 12 hours. Drain the rice and place in a covered steamer over medium low heat for 50 minutes or until rice is cooked. Transfer the rice to a large bowl and fluff it with a fork.

In a medium bowl, combine the coconut milk, sugar, and salt. Stir until the sugar dissolves. Add and mix in the still-warm cooked rice and let sit for 30 minutes. Cut each piece of mango into lengthwise slices. Mound the rice in the center each dessert plate and arrange the slices of mango around it. Pour the coconut rum over the rice and serve.

Mango Split with Rum-Caramel Sauce and Macadamia Nuts

This delicious dessert is a tropical mango split with a hot sauce of diced mango, macadamia nuts, and caramel. It will bring out the kid in you.

Serves 4

  2 large ripe mangos, peeled and cut from the pit
  $1/4$ cup packed brown sugar
  1 tablespoon unsalted butter
  1 tablespoon freshly squeezed lime juice
  $1/8$ teaspoon ground cinnamon
  1 tablespoon dark rum
  1 pint Mango Sorbet (page 123)
  1 pint vanilla ice cream
  $1/2$ cup sweetened whipped cream
  $1/2$ cup macadamia nuts
  2 tablespoons shredded coconut, toasted (see note)

Cut 3 of the mango cheeks into 2-inch-thick wedges. Cut the remaining cheek and side flesh into $1/2$-inch dice. In a small saucepan, combine the brown sugar, butter, lime juice, and cinnamon. Cook over medium heat, stirring, until the mixture turns into a smooth caramel. Mix in the diced mango, and simmer for 2 minutes. Remove from heat and stir in the rum.

Using 4 shallow soup bowls or coupe dishes, add 2 scoops of mango sorbet and 1 scoop of vanilla ice cream to each. Divide the mango wedges around the ice cream. Spoon the warm caramel sauce over the top. Garnish with whipped cream, macadamia nuts, and coconut.

Toasting Coconut: Preheat the oven to 325°. Spread the coconut on a small baking sheet. Bake the coconut for 5 to 6 minutes then turn and mix the flakes. Return to the oven for another 3 to 4 minutes, until golden brown.

Mango Crème Brûlée with Lavender-Nut Fricassee

I like to use a sweet-tart mango, such as the Carabao or the Edward, in this creamy, rich dessert, but any ripe mango will do.

Serves 6

- 4 large egg yolks
- $1/4$ cup sugar
- $2^1/2$ cups heavy cream
- 1 vanilla bean, split lengthwise
- 1 large, ripe mango, peeled, cut from the pit, and cut into $1/2$ -inch dice

LAVENDER-NUT FRICASSEE

- $1/3$ cup pine nuts
- $1/3$ cup pistachio nuts
- $1/3$ cup pecans
- $1/3$ cup sugar
- $3/4$ teaspoon ground cinnamon
- 1 teaspoon ground cardamom
- 1 tablespoon dried lavender
- $1/2$ teaspoon minced fresh mint
- $1/4$ cup diced dried figs
- $1/4$ cup raisins
- 2 tablespoons packed light brown sugar

In a medium bowl, whisk the egg yolks and sugar together until smooth. In a medium saucepan, combine the cream and vanilla bean. Heat over medium heat until bubbles form around the edges of the pan. Gradually whisk the cream into the egg mixture. Set the custard aside.

Preheat the oven to 300°. Divide the mango among six 4-ounce ramekins. Strain the custard through a fine-mesh sieve and pour over the mango. Place the ramekins in a baking pan and add hot water to come halfway up the sides of the ramekins. Carefully place the pan in the oven and bake for about 40 minutes, or until just set. Remove from the oven and carefully set ramekins aside to cool for at least 1 hour. Refrigerate for at least 2 hours or up to 24 hours.

To make the fricassee: Preheat the oven to 350°. Spread all the nuts on a rimmed baking sheet and toast for 4 to 5 minutes. Remove from the oven and transfer to a small bowl. While still warm, add the sugar and toss to coat the nuts. Add the spices, mint and dried fruits. Return to the oven for 5 minutes. Let cool.

Preheat the broiler. Sprinkle each custard evenly with 1 teaspoon brown sugar pushed through a sieve. Place under the broiler, about 2 inches from the heat source, for 1 to 2 minutes, or until the sugar has melted and browned. Cool slightly then garnish with the fricassee and serve.

Mango Leather

Mango leather, like peach leather, is a great treat, and one that children love.

Makes one 14 inch roll, approximately

> **2 pounds ripe mangos, peeled, cut from the pit, and coarsely chopped**
> **1 tablespoon freshly squeezed lemon juice**
> **3 tablespoons sugar**

Preheat the oven to 225°. In a food processor purée the mangos until smooth. Add the lemon juice and sugar. Purée until the sugar is dissolved.

Dampen a rimmed pan and line it with sheets of plastic film large enough to overlap the edges. Pour the mango mixture onto the lined pan. By tipping and tilting the tray, spread it out into an even layer about 1/4 inch thick.

Place in the oven for 12 to 14 hours, or until dry but pliable. Remove from the oven and cool.

Peel the leather off the plastic film and transfer to a sheet of waxed paper. Roll the leather up into a cylinder. Store in an airtight container for up to 2 weeks.

Mango Gingersnaps

Ginger and mango is an inviting combination in both sweet and savory preparations. Try these gingersnaps right out of the oven.

Makes about 3 dozen

- 1 large ripe mango, peeled, cut from the pit, and chopped
- 2 teaspoons ground ginger
- 1/2 teaspoon ground cinnamon
- 1/4 teaspoon ground cloves
- 3/4 cup (1 1/2 sticks) unsalted butter, at room temperature
- 2 1/2 cups sugar
- 2 large eggs
- 3 3/4 cups unbleached all-purpose flour
- 1 1/2 teaspoons baking soda
- Pinch of salt

Preheat the oven to 350°. Line a baking sheet with parchment paper. In a food processor, purée the mango until smooth. In a small saucepan, combine 3/4 cup of the mango purée, the ginger, cinnamon, and cloves. Bring to a simmer and cook, stirring frequently so the mango does not scorch on the bottom of the pan, for 5 minutes, or until thickened. Remove from heat and let cool.

In a medium bowl, cream the butter and 2 cups of the sugar together until light and fluffy. Beat the eggs, one at a time, into the butter mixture. In a small bowl, stir the flour, salt, and baking soda together. Fold half of the flour mixture into the batter. Stir in the mango mixture. Fold in the remaining flour mixture.

Scoop the cookie mixture into walnut-sized balls and roll them individually in the remaining 1/2 cup sugar. Place the balls 2 inches apart on the prepared pan and flatten slightly with the prongs of a fork. Bake for 10 minutes, until golden brown. Remove from the oven and let cool slightly before transferring from the pan to wire racks.

Mango Cheesecake

The lush creaminess of cheesecake is a perfect foil for a rich, complex-tasting mango. The Bombay mango would be wonderful here. Serve with sliced mango for additional texture and flavor.

Serves 10

> 2 large ripe mangos, peeled, cut from the pit, and chopped
> 1¼ cups sugar
> 1½ pounds cream cheese, at room temperature
> 6 large eggs, lightly beaten

Preheat the oven to 300°. Line the bottom of a buttered 10-inch springform pan with a round of waxed paper. Butter the paper and the sides of the pan. Sprinkle the sides and base of the pan with ¼ cup of the sugar.

In a food processor, purée the mango until smooth. Pass the purée through a fine-mesh sieve into a bowl. You should have at least 3 cups purée.

In the bowl of a mixer fitted with the paddle attachment, beat the cream cheese until smooth.

Add the remaining 1 cup sugar, and continue to beat on medium speed until completely incorporated. Add and beat in the mango purée. Add the eggs into the mango mixture, with the motor running, in 3 parts, scraping down the bowl between each addition.

Wrap the bottom of the springform pan with aluminum foil to keep it from leaking. Pour the batter into the pan and place into a larger baking pan. Add water to come halfway up the sides of the springform pan. Bake for about 1½ hours, or until firm. Test the center with a small knife point to see that it comes out clean. Remove from the oven and let cool completely on a wire rack. Cover and refrigerate overnight. Remove from springform pan before serving.

BIBLIOGRAPHY

Achaya, K. T. *Indian Food: A Historical Companion*. Delhi, India: Oxford University Press. 1994.

Campbell, Richard. *Mangos: A Guide to Mangos in Florida*. Miami, Fla.: Fairchild Tropical Gardens, 1992.

Lynch, S. John, and Margaret J. Mustard, *Mangos in Florida*. Tallahasee, Fla.: Department of Agriculture.

Nair, Thankappan P. *The Mango in Indian Life and Culture*. Dehra Dan, India: Bishen Singh Mahendra Pal Singh, 1996.

Pope, W. T. *Mango Culture in Hawaii*. Honolulu: Hawaii Agricultural Experiment Station. Bulletin no. 58 (1929).

Popenoe, F. W. *The Mango in Southern California*. Altadena, Calif.: Pomona College of Economic Botany, 1911.

Rawlings, Marjorie Kinnan. *Cross Creek Cookery*. New York: Charles Scribner's Sons, 1942.

Rolfs, P.H. *Mangos in Florida*. Gainesville, Fla.: University of Florida Agricultural Experiment Station. Bulletin no. 127 (1915).

Singh, Lal Behari. *The Mango: Botany, Cultivation, and Utilization*. London: Leonard Hill Books Ltd., 1960.

Sturrock, David. "Notes on the Mango," *Stuart Daily News*, 1944.

Webster, P.J. *The Mango Bulletin*. Manila, Philippine Islands: Department of Public Instruction, Bureau of Agriculture. Bulletin no. 18 (1911).

INDEX

A

Achar (Green Mango Pickle), 110
Ah Ping, 2
Alampur Baneshan, 2
Ale-Roasted Pompano with a
    Mango-Cashew Salsa, 96–97
Alexander the Great, x
Almond and Mango Macaroon
    Tart, 126
Alphonse (Alphonso), 4, 120, 123
Anderson, 4
Ataulfo, 6, 10, 115
Australia, 30, 44
Avocado and Mango Salad, 85

B

Banana, Mango, and Pistachio
    Strudel, 120
Bangkok, xv
Baptiste, 6
Barbados, x
Beans
    Mango and Avocado Salad, 85
Beef
    Thai Steak and Mango Salad, 77
Bet Dagan, Israel, 22
Beverages
    Chef Allen's Mango Martini, 70
    Mango Daiquiri, 70
    Mango Frappé, 71
    Mango Lassi, 71
    Mango Vodka, 70
Bombay, 8
Botanical classification, x, xiii–xiv
Brazil, x, xii, xvi, 44, 48
Broward County, Florida, 52
Butter, clarifying, 91

C

Cake, Mango Sour Cream
    Crumb, 121
Calcutta, x
Cambodiana, 8, 105
Carabao, xi, xv, 10, 14, 83
Cashews
    Dried-Fruit Chutney, 113
    Mango-Cashew Salsa, 96–97
Cheesecake, Mango, 135

Chef Allen's Mango Martini, 70
Chicken
    Chicken and Green Mango Stew,
        100–101
    Creole Fried Chicken with
        Mango, 94
    Mango-Braised Drumsticks, 84
China, x, 24, 38, 46
Chow, Mango, 114
Chutneys
    Dried-Fruit Chutney, 113
    Green Mango Chutney, 107
    Quick Ripe-Mango Chutney, 106
    Raw-Mango Chutney, 105
Cobbler, Mango, 127
Coconut, toasting, 130
Coconut Grove, Florida, 18, 30, 54
Coconut milk
    Chicken and Green Mango Stew,
        100–101
    Crab and Mango Salad, 80–81
    Mangos with Sticky Rice, 129
    Shrimp and Mango Curry, 74
Colombia, 48, 56
Colors, xiv, xvii
Country Mango Tarts, 125
Crab
    Crab and Mango Salad, 80–81
    Panfried Soft-Shell Crabs with
        Green Mango Slaw, 95
Cream cheese
    Country Mango Tarts, 125
    Mango Cheesecake, 135
Crème Brûlée, Mango, with
    Lavender-Nut Fricassee,
    132–33
Creole Fried Chicken with
    Mango, 94
Cuba, xii, 46, 52
Cucumber
    Mango and Avocado Salad, 85
    Mango-Shrimp Cocktail, 79
    Mango-Shrimp Salsa, 89
Cultivation, x, xiii–xv
Cumin seeds, toasting, 93
Curry, Shrimp and Mango, 74
Cushman, 10
Cutting technique, 64

D

Daiquiri, Mango, 70
Dasheri, 12, 34, 123
Dates
    Dried-Fruit Chutney, 113
    Green Mango Chutney, 107
Delray Beach, Florida, 20
Desserts
    Country Mango Tarts, 125
    Ginger-Rum Grilled Pineapple
        with Mango Sorbet, 122–23
    Indian Mango Ice Cream, 128
    Mango and Almond Macaroon
        Tart, 126
    Mango, Banana, and Pistachio
        Strudel, 120
    Mango Cheesecake, 135
    Mango Cobbler, 127
    Mango Crème Brûlée with
        Lavender-Nut Fricassee,
        132–33
    Mango Gingersnaps, 134
    Mango Leather, 133
    Mango Sorbet, 123
    Mango Sour Cream Crumb
        Cake, 121
    Mango Split with Rum-Caramel
        Sauce and Macadamia
        Nuts, 130
    Mangos with Sticky Rice, 129
Diplomatico, 12
Dried-Fruit Chutney, 113
Drying technique, 80

E, F

East Indian, 14
Edward, 14, 127
Fairchild, David, xii, 8
Festivals, xii
Figs
    Lavender-Nut Fricassee, 132–33
Fish
    Ale-Roasted Pompano with a
        Mango-Cashew Salsa, 96–97
    Grilled Mahimahi with Mango
        Sauce and Mango-Shrimp
        Salsa, 88–89
    Seared Herb-Coated Tuna with
        Saffron-Macadamia-Mango
        Rice, 90–91
    Tuna and Mango Sashimi
        Salad, 83
Flagler, Henry, xii

Florida, xii, xvi, 4, 8, 10, 16, 18, 20,
    22, 24, 26, 28, 30, 36, 40, 44, 48,
    52, 54, 56, 58, 115
Florigon, 16
Ft. Lauderdale, 16
Frappé, Mango, 71

G

Gale, Elbridge, 36
Ginger-Rum Grilled Pineapple
    with Mango Sorbet, 122–23
Gingersnaps, Mango, 134
Glaze, Spicy Mango, 101
Glenn, 16
Glenn, Roscoe E., 16
Goa, India, 4, 48, 50
Golek, 18
Green mangos
    Chicken and Green Mango
        Stew, 100–101
    Dried-Fruit Chutney, 113
    Green Mango Chutney, 107
    Green Mango Pickle (Achar), 110
    Green Mango Raita, 93
    Green Mango Slaw, 111
    Hot and Sour Mango
        Relish, 104
    immature vs. mature, 62
    Lamb Chops with Dried Mango
        and Ginger, 92–93
    Mango Souscaille with
        Prosciutto, 73
    Raw-Mango Chutney, 105
    Shrimp and Mango Curry, 74
Grilled Mahimahi with Mango
    Sauce and Mango-Shrimp
    Salsa, 88–89

H

Haden, xii, xvi, 2, 14, 18, 36, 84
Haden, Capt. F. O., 18
Haiti, 6, 32
Hawaii, xi, 2
Hedgehog technique, 65
History, x
Homestead, Florida, 28
Hot and Sour Mango Relish, 104

I

Ice cream
    Indian Mango Ice Cream, 128
    Mango Frappé, 71
    Mango Split with Rum-Caramel
        Sauce and Macadamia
        Nuts, 130

India, x, xi, xii, xvii, 2, 4, 8, 12, 34, 36, 38, 48, 50, 107, 110, 128
Indian Mango Ice Cream, 128
Indonesia, 18
Indus Valley, x
Iris, 20
Irwin, 20, 24, 127
Israel, xvii, 14, 38
  BD 20-26, 22
  BD 34-80, 22
  13-1, 20
Ivory, 24

J

Jakarta, 26
Jam, Mango, 115
Jamaica, x–xi, xvii, 8, 14, 28, 40, 114
Japan, 40, 46
Jewel, 26
Julie, xi, 28

K

Kama Sutra, xvii
Keitt, 28, 44, 50
Keitt, Mrs. J. N., 28
Kensington, 30
Kent, 30, 36, 107
Kent, Leith D., 30
Ketchup, Mango, 117
Kulfi, 128
Kyo Savoy, 32, 100, 104

L

Lake Worth, Florida, 36, 58
Lamb Chops with Dried Mango and Ginger, 92–93
Lassi, Mango, 71
Lavender-Nut Fricassee, 132–33
Leather, Mango, 133
Lobster
  Lobster and Mango Salad, 72
  Pan-Roasted Lobster with Spicy Mango Glaze, 101

M

Macadamia nuts
  Ginger-Rum Grilled Pineapple with Mango Sorbet, 122–23
  Mango Split with Rum-Caramel Sauce and Macadamia Nuts, 130
  Saffron-Macadamia-Mango Rice, 91
  toasting, 122

Madame Francis, 32
Mahimahi, Grilled, with Mango Sauce and Mango-Shrimp Salsa, 88–89
Malay Archipelago, x
Malaysia, xii
Mallika, 34
Mangiferi indica, x
Mango and Almond Macaroon Tart, 126
Mango and Avocado Salad, 85
Mango and Papaya Salsa, 112
Mango, Banana, and Pistachio Strudel, 120
Mango-Braised Drumsticks, 84
Mango-Cashew Salsa, 96–97
Mango Cheesecake, 135
Mango Chow, 114
Mango Cobbler, 127
Mango Crème Brûlée with Lavender-Nut Fricassee, 132–33
Mango Daiquiri, 70
Mango Frappé, 71
Mango Gingersnaps, 134
Mango Jam, 115
Mango Ketchup, 117
Mango Lassi, 71
Mango Leather, 133
Mango Mojo, 109
Mango-Peach Marmalade, 116
Mango Sauce, 88
Mango-Shrimp Cocktail, 79
Mango-Shrimp Salsa, 89
Mango Sorbet, 123
Mango Sour Cream Crumb Cake, 121
Mango Souscaille with Prosciutto, 73
Mango Split with Rum-Caramel Sauce and Macadamia Nuts, 130
Mangos with Sticky Rice, 129
Mango Vinaigrette, 108
Mango Vodka, 70
Manila (city), xv–xvi
Manila (variety), 8, 34, 120
Manzanillo, 36
Manzano. *See* Vallenato
Marmalade, Mango-Peach, 116
Martini, Chef Allen's Mango, 70
Merritt Island, Florida, 44
Mexico, xi, 6, 12, 34, 36, 42, 114
Miami, xii, 4, 8, 10, 14, 16, 24, 48

Miami Plant Introduction
    Garden, xii
Mojo, Mango, 109
Mulgoba, xii, 18, 36

n
Nam Doc Mai, 40, 46, 54, 100
Naomi, 38
Neelum, 34, 38
Number 11, xi, xii, xvii, 40

O
Okrong Tong, 42, 54
Oro, 42
Osteen, 44

P
Paheri, 8
Pakistan, 50
Palmer, 44
Panfried Soft-Shell Crabs with
    Green Mango Slaw, 95
Pan-Roasted Lobster with Spicy
    Mango Glaze, 101
Papaya and Mango Salsa, 112
Peach-Mango Marmalade, 116
Pecans
    Lavender-Nut Fricassee, 132–33
    Mango Sour Cream Crumb
        Cake, 121
Perrine, Henry, xi
Peru, 14
Philippines, x, xi, xv–xvi, 8, 10, 34
Phimsen Mun. See Rad
Pickle, Green Mango (Achar), 110
Pineapple, Ginger-Rum Grilled,
    with Mango Sorbet, 122–23
Pirie, xi, 8
Pistachio nuts
    Indian Mango Ice Cream, 128
    Lavender-Nut Fricassee, 132–33
    Mango, Banana, and Pistachio
        Strudel, 120
Plantains
    Chicken and Green Mango Stew,
        100–101
    Roast Pork Loin with Mango
        Mojo and Yellow Plantains, 99
Pompano, Ale-Roasted, with a
    Mango-Cashew Salsa, 96–97
Pork Loin, Roast, with Mango
    Mojo and Yellow Plantains, 99
Potatoes
    Chicken and Green Mango Stew,
        100–101

Prieto, 46
Prosciutto, Mango Souscaille
    with, 73

Q, R
Quick Ripe-Mango Chutney, 106
Rad, 46
Raisins
    Dried-Fruit Chutney, 113
    Green Mango Chutney, 107
    Lavender-Nut Fricassee, 132–33
    Quick Ripe-Mango Chutney, 106
Raita, Green Mango, 93
Rat. See Rad
Raw-Mango Chutney, 105
Rehovot, Israel, 22
Religious symbolism, x
Relish, Hot and Sour Mango, 104
Rice
    Mangos with Sticky Rice, 129
    Saffron-Macadamia-Mango
        Rice, 91
Ripening, 62–63
Roast Pork Loin with Mango Mojo
    and Yellow Plantains, 99
Rosa, 48
Ruby, 48

S
Sabre, 50
Saffron-Macadamia-Mango
    Rice, 91
Salads
    Crab and Mango Salad, 80–81
    Green Mango Slaw, 111
    Lobster and Mango Salad, 72
    Mango and Avocado Salad, 85
    Thai Steak and Mango Salad, 77
    Tuna and Mango Sashimi
        Salad, 83
Salsas
    Mango and Papaya Salsa, 112
    Mango-Cashew Salsa, 96–97
    Mango Chow, 114
    Mango-Shrimp Salsa, 89
Sandersha, 50
Sauces. See also Salsas
    Mango Mojo, 109
    Mango Sauce, 88
Scallops, Spice-Rubbed Jumbo,
    with Mango and Papaya
        Salsa, 78
Seared Herb-Coated Tuna with
    Saffron-Macadamia-Mango
        Rice, 90–91

Selection tips, 62–63
Sesame seeds, toasting, 83
Shrimp
  Hot and Sour Mango Relish, 104
  Mango-Shrimp Cocktail, 79
  Mango-Shrimp Salsa, 89
  Shrimp and Mango Curry, 74
Simmonds, Edward, 14
Slaw, Green Mango, 111
Sorbet
  Mango Sorbet, 123
  Mango Split with Rum-Caramel
    Sauce and Macadamia
    Nuts, 130
South Africa, xii, 44
Species name, x
Spice-Rubbed Jumbo Scallops
    with Mango and Papaya
    Salsa, 78
Spicy Mango Glaze, 101
Squash
  Chicken and Green Mango Stew,
    100–101
Storing, 62, 63
Strudel, Mango, Banana, and
    Pistachio, 120
Sweet potatoes
  Chicken and Green Mango Stew,
    100–101
  Shrimp and Mango Curry, 74

T
Taiwan, 24
Tarts
  Country Mango Tarts, 125
  Mango and Almond Macaroon
    Tart, 126
Thailand, xv, 24, 32, 40, 42, 46, 54
Thai Steak and Mango Salad, 77

Toledo, 52
Tomatoes
  Mango and Avocado Salad, 85
  Mango-Cashew Salsa, 96–97
Tommy Atkins, xvi, 44, 52, 84
Tong Dam, 54
Trinidad, 114
Tuna
  Seared Herb-Coated Tuna with
    Saffron-Macadamia-Mango
    Rice, 90–91
  Tuna and Mango Sashimi
    Salad, 83
Turpentine, 20, 54, 84

V
Valencia Pride, 56
Vallenato, 56
Van Dyke, 58
Vatsyayana, xvii
Vietnam, xvi, 104
Vinaigrette, Mango, 108
Vodka, Mango, 70

W, Y, Z
Watermelon
  Mango-Shrimp Cocktail, 79
  Mango-Shrimp Salsa, 89
Yogurt
  Green Mango Raita, 93
  Mango Lassi, 71
Yuca
  Chicken and Green Mango Stew,
    100–101
Yucatán, 6
Zill, 58
Zill, Lawrence, 58

OTHER GREAT BOOKS
FROM TEN SPEED PRESS

The Great Exotic Fruit Book
by Norman Van Aken
and John Harrison
$15.95 (Can $25.50), 160 pages,
ISBN 0-89815-688-2

The Great Salsa Book
by Mark Miller with Mark Kiffin
and John Harrison
$14.95 (Can $23.95), 160 pages,
ISBN 0-89815-517-7

The Great Margarita Book
by Al Lucero with John Harrison
$15.95 (Can $25.50), 160 pages,
ISBN 1-58008-053-7

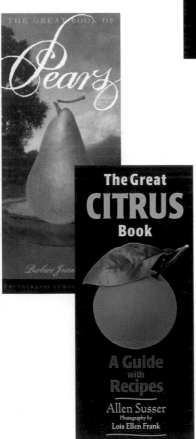

The Great Book of Pears
by Barbara Flores
$16.95 (Can $26.95), 176 pages,
ISBN 1-58008-036-7

The Great Citrus Book
by Allen Susser
$16.95 (Can $26.95), 160 pages,
ISBN 0-89815-855-9